Miracles In My Life

Autobiography of Adventist Pioneer
J.N. Loughborough

TEACH Services, Inc.
P U B L I S H I N G
www.TEACHServices.com • (800) 367-1844

Copyright © 2014 TEACH Services, Inc.
ISBN-13: 978-1-4796-0290-2 (Paperback)
ISBN-13: 978-1-4796-0291-9 (ePub)
ISBN-13: 978-1-4796-0292-6 (mobi)
Library of Congress Control Number: 2014933548

Published by

TEACH Services, Inc.
P U B L I S H I N G
www.TEACHServices.com • (800) 367-1844

A Flash Ahead

Madam Parrot never dreamed that her decision to ride side-saddle to the tent meeting would draw the attention of the entire community. Nor did she foresee her near-fatal accident and her healing so miraculous that even atheists could not deny.

Among those who attended John Loughborough's evangelistic meetings at Santa Rosa was a young medical graduate from Geneva known as Madam Parrot. An urgent sick call took her to the bedside of Mrs. Skinner at Piner. After a week's cot-duty, her patient had so recovered that Dr. Parrot announced her intention to return to the tent meetings. Mrs. Skinner's atheist son Oliver readied a horse that was used to ladies, but as she mounted, he began to buck furiously.

She was thrown to the ground and the horse upon her with such force that it bent the saddle horn out straight. As her friends looked upon her mangled form, they felt certain she was dead. When she regained consciousness, she could barely whisper.

"Shall we send for a doctor?" someone asked her.

"No," she responded. "A doctor can do me no good. Send for the ministers at the tent. If they pray for me, the Lord will heal me."

Elders Loughborough and Bourdeau had just begun their evening meeting when the prayer request reached them. Thinking it unwise to dismiss their congregation, they promised to come very early the next morning. When they arrived, they learned that the doctor's condition had required four attendants throughout the night.

"Anoint me and pray, and the Lord will heal me," she whispered.

As the ministers prayed, Dr. Parrot soon began to pray in a loud voice, then clapped her hands and declared, "I am healed!" She arose, dressed herself, and began to assist with the home duties. In the evening she rode to the meeting in a lumber wagon, completely free from all pain. Former atheist Oliver now enthusiastically witnessed of God's power to everyone he met.

John Norton Loughborough
1832 – 1924

Table of Contents

Chapter 1

My Early Years

Many have requested me to give some remembrances of early times, and manifestations of the Lord's dealings with His people. Having been familiar with the Advent movement of 1843–144, and having since January 2, 1849 proclaimed the doctrine, I esteem it a pleasure to "speak the things which I have seen and heard." I will first call attention to some things in my own early life.

I was born in Victor, Ontario County, New York, January 26, 1832. My father was an earnest, local Methodist preacher. When I was three years of age, a Miss Bibbins started a school for little tots in one of the classrooms of the Methodist Church. On the last day of school we were all taken into the sanctuary where our parents and others were assembled to hear recitations. Among the rest, I was called upon to make my first public speech, which consisted of a bit of poetry I had learned. When the people clapped their hands, I did not know it had any reference to what I had done, so supposed it to be their part of the meeting.

In our childhood days our parents took us little folks to the "love feasts" and the communion seasons of the church. I well remember that as testimonies were borne in those love feasts, they were moistened with tears and accompanied with shouts of praise that touched our young hearts. I remember, too, how plainly the people dressed—neatly, yet without any display of jewelry.

In those days, those who were to partake of communion received a ticket from the class leader. One woman did not get a ticket because she had worn gold. Shortly afterward, her daughter was excluded from church for attending a ball. Poor girl! She took a violent cold as the result of a night of dancing, sickened and died. At her funeral the minister expressed some doubts as to her acceptance with the Lord.

We children learned the do, re, mi, from the choir leader who always started the singing with a tuning fork. As he placed this to his ear, he would sound the do; then those of the other parts of the music would sound their first note before singing.

There came a time when a man stood at the head of the choir with a violin with which to give the leading note. Though it was a decided improvement, it displeased some of the members who thought that no instrumental music should be used in the Lord's house. They thought the violin's only use was "with the devil's music in dance halls."

Once when my father was constructing a certain house, there was quite a large pile of stones which they wanted moved to the other side of the fence. My uncle, who was one of the carpenters, said if I would move them with my little wheelbarrow, I would find a sixpence (twelve and one-half cents) under the last stone. Of course I worked hard to get to the last stone, and sure enough, there was the sixpence. I knew very well that my uncle had to divert my attention just before I picked up that last stone.

The interesting thing is the use I made of that sixpence. At that time the Methodists were carrying on missionary work on the west coast of Africa. My sympathies were aroused, and I decided that my sixpence should buy a Testament for some poor heathen boy. There was to be a meeting at the minister's house that week for the people to bring clothing, money, etc. to send to Africa. The day of the missionary meeting I was sent to the store for some article. Whether to test me or not, the merchant showed me some things he knew I loved, and offered to sell them for a sixpence. There was a struggle within me whether to buy the articles or not. Then I thought of the poor heathen and left the store on a run. I hurried to the minister's house just as the people were gathering, and handed him the sixpence saying, "I want to send a Testament to the poor heathen." Then I left for home as suddenly as I had come. As I went out, I saw the minister holding up the sixpence and talking to the people. Some of them shed tears. I imagine he made my sixpence tell for more than twelve and one-half cents. I know that I felt very happy afterwards.

In the winter of 1837, the night after my sixth birthday, a terrific sight appeared in the heavens and continued for the whole night. It was the fiery aurora. A man and his wife living directly across from our home had taken my father and mother for a sleigh ride to spend the evening with another family two miles away. Two girls from the neighbor's family and a Miss Horton, 18 years of age, came to spend the evening with us children. About seven o'clock, while we were enjoying our childish sports, there came a sudden flash of red light. My brother cried out, "The house is afire!" and we all rushed out-of-doors. What a sight greeted our eyes! The whole heavens had the appearance of a red flame, mingled with cloudy vapor. The reflection of this upon the snow appeared like fire rolling in waves down from the hillside.

Even Miss Horton was startled and cried out, "The world is coming to an end!" Our parents, who anticipated our terror, were soon home to calm our fright. Some of the neighbors sat up all night to watch the ever-changing grandeur. The aurora was seen all over the then settled portions of the United States.

During the summer of 1839, my father had seventeen men in his employ. In addition to his cabinet and chair business, he built houses and constructed horse powers for threshing machines. He was also the only coffin-maker for a large section of the surrounding country. Besides giving attention to all his business, he spent nearly every Sunday holding meetings in the Methodist Church. Sometimes on arriving home at eleven o'clock at night, he would find an order for a coffin which must be had the next day, and the rest of the night must be spent in making it.

Notwithstanding he was a man of vigorous constitution, and only 35 years of age, it is no marvel that in September he was confined to his bed with typhoid fever, with little vital force remaining to expel the disease from his system. Those were the days of bleeding and dosing with calomel for every affliction. A patient was not allowed any water or fresh air. When I think of how my father was served by a physician of that time, it is no wonder that he died. My father's funeral was attended by about 2,000 people, nearly all mourners. Dearly did I love my father! As I saw him covered up in the cold ground, I began to realize that I could see him no more. With a sad heart I went to make my home with my grandfather who was a Methodist class leader.

What the different ministers said at other funerals I attended about this time brought me both joy and sadness. I distinctly remember one prominent minister saying that the saints in heaven would sit on the edge of a cloud and sing psalm tunes forever. Not having any idea how far it was to heaven, I fancied it might be that some of those beautiful, shining, fleecy clouds of summer piled up like bales of purest wool appeared so glorious because the saints were on them. Many an hour did I sit watching these clouds and wondering if I could hear them sing. But alas! they always seemed to stay on the other side of the cloud. At a funeral I attended six months later, the minister declared the soul to be immortal and invisible, and so small that 3,000 could dance on the point of a needle. This sadly destroyed my childish fancy about the bright clouds.

Although my grandparents believed the coming of the Lord to be near, they also believed we were to "occupy till I come," so they wished me to get a good education. Not only was I anxious to secure education from books, but also in the use of tools. A cousin of mine had a violin. Since I had no money to purchase one, I made one, shaping the bulge of the instrument from a beech board. I never became a violinist. A physician in the village, to encourage me, paid me a good price for the instrument for it was a careful copy of those sold in music stores.

As I began to study "Comstock's Philosophy," I wanted to make everything described in the book. I constructed an electrical machine with its glass cylinder for generating electricity, the Leyden jar with thunder tongs, dancing jacks, hair-raising images, and other paraphernalia. Then I made a galvanic battery of copper and zinc, with a rasp electric coil for administering electrical shocks. I did not consider the making of these things any great feat, but soon I was branded "the philosopher" and was even called to administer, for pay, electric treatments to a paralytic.

In my grandfather's household, in addition to butchering a cow each fall, they killed three fat hogs. From these came the meat supply for a year. Of course, the fresh beef was the diet for a very few days, and after that corned beef and dried smoked beef. The pork was the standard diet, and all the fat used freely in shortcake, pie-crust, etc.

Flesh food was a staple article of diet three times a day. Fried pork with Java coffee for breakfast, boiled pork for dinner, and if baked beans were a part of the fare, they were not considered ready without a nice piece of pork on top. For supper we had dried beef or ham, and shortcake so full of lard you could almost squeeze out the grease. For appetizers we had mustard, pickles, horseradish, and good sharp cider vinegar.

Grandfather was a devout Christian and lived his religion before his fellow men. It was not popular in those days to be a Methodist, and some of our Universalist neighbors resorted to ridicule and petty annoyances. As we would come home from church, we would sometimes find several lengths of fence pulled down and the cattle in the grain field. Grandfather well knew who did the mischief for he would see them sneering as he drove out the cattle and put up the fence on Sunday, but he said nothing. One summer day as the family came home, grandfather was astonished to see his fine cherry trees stripped of large limbs of ripe cherries. Many weeks later they were discovered a half-mile away in a deep woods. Grandfather said nothing, but prayed for his enemies.

Amid all these perplexing incidents grandfather sought for grace to bear persecution without complaining, often using a favorite expression, "It's a long road that doesn't have a turn in it." He expected there would be a respite after a while, and at last it came in a very peculiar manner. On the back side of his farm was a long, ten-acre field of wheat, nearly ripe. His enemies thought to spite him by cutting the wheat before it was fully ripe, supposing it would shrink and be greatly damaged. So on Sunday, while the family was at the meeting three miles away, these enemies went in and cut the whole ten acres and laid it nicely in swaths.

Little did they realize that they had done him a favor instead of a curse. Grandfather had decided that year to cut his wheat before it was ripe enough to shell. Unknown to his enemies he had engaged two men to come on Monday to help harvest that field of wheat. What was their surprise to find the whole ten acres neatly laid in swaths!

With a smile grandfather said, "Well, I think the devil overshot his mark this time." As a result of the early cutting, his wheat was the finest in the neighborhood. That ended all opposition from those people. In his last days, let anyone say a word against Nathan Loughborough and those former opponents were ready to speak of his merits.

Chapter 2

A Time For Decision

As we went to meeting one Sunday in December, 1843, my sister said to me, "Oh John, aren't you glad! The millennium is going to begin this year!"

"What's the millennium?" I asked her. I had never heard that big word before.

"Well," she began, "the world is coming to an end, and Jesus will return. The wicked will be destroyed and the earth will become like it was when God first made it."

"How do you know?" I asked.

"The Bible teaches it," she replied. "There is a man by the name of Adams coming here this week to preach about it, and we are going to hear him."

The news didn't please me as it did her. Grandfather sent me around the neighborhood to spread the news. Many of the neighbors looked sad, and I felt sad enough, too, for I thought I was unready and would have to burn eternally in hell for my sins.

After Elder Adams' lectures, a second series was given by Elder Barry. Victor was then only a small town of 300 inhabitants, but the Methodist Church comfortably seated 1,000. It was not only full every evening, but all standing room was taken. These lectures on the prophecies and signs of the times, mingled with exhortations to seek God, created a profound interest.

I was able to attend one of Elder Barry's lectures. It was a beautiful night and fine for sleighing. The meeting was opened by the singing of a peculiar hymn. In a clear and musical voice there came from one corner of the room the words, "Hail you! and where do you come from?" From the opposite corner a melodious response, "I am come from the land of Egypt." Then the question, "Hail you! and where are you bound for?" followed by the reply, "I am bound for the land of Canaan." Then a full choir of all parts gave the chorus—

"O Canaan, bright Canaan!
I am bound for the land of Canaan.
O Canaan, it is my happy home;
I am bound for the land of Canaan."

Then in the same manner came questions relative to captain, pilot, cargo, etc. Simple as were these words, the power of God filled the place, and the people were in tears.

Elder Barry spoke from Revelation 14, "Fear God and give glory to Him for the hour of His judgment is come." Above and back of the pulpit hung a chart of the imagery of the books of Daniel and Revelation. Oh, what solemn awe seemed to prevail! Although the church was filled to capacity, all listened with breathless attention. At the close of the sermon, scores went forward for prayers. I took my place among the seekers, desirous to be ready to meet the Lord in peace.

Afterwards, one man said to me, "Well, Johnnie, I'm glad you've decided to be a good boy." I felt disappointed. I longed for someone to help me seek and find the favor of the dreadful, angry God I pictured in my mind, who would be pleased to destroy me. I was not quite twelve years of age.

As we came out of the church, we were strangely awed by a band of white light about as wide as the moon's disk stretched across the heavens from southwest to northeast. That wonderful band of light continued all that night and the whole of the next night.

As a result of the lectures my grandfather and his whole family, with hundreds of others, believed the doctrine. They used to bring home books and papers such as *Signs of the Times*, and *Voice of Truth*. I read them eagerly and carried them to the neighbors. A great revival followed the preaching of the Advent doctrine.

The first time that was set for the Lord to come (in the spring of 1844), I worked all the day the Lord was expected, sawing wood. I frequently looked up to see if the Lord was coming. I was very fearful He would come that day, for I thought I was not ready. Although the day passed and He did not come, I did not lose my desire to be saved.

In April 1847, at the age of fifteen, I left my grandparent's home and went to my native village to live with my oldest brother who was an Adventist. I wanted to learn the trade of carriage-making. Here I soon mixed with wild companions and became very careless about religion. When I stopped to think seriously and wished to be good, I was of the same mind as my brother; but I had no strength to leave my companions and make a start to serve the Lord. During the winter of 1848–49, I attended the school in Victor, living with my widowed mother, paying my school tuition by sweeping the school floor, kindling the morning fires, and ringing the bell.

Our teacher readily discerned the abilities of his students and did all he could to develop them. He had the more advanced students organize a literary society. The older male members were required to write speeches, commit them to memory, and present them before the assembly. This trained us to appear in public. I can look back and see that the Lord was preparing me to speak on Bible truths.

When my mother would ask me to go to meeting on Sunday, I would make up some excuse—my studies needed attention, I must write a composition, or something of the kind. Thus things went until June when I accompanied my Uncle Norton to visit my older brother who had moved to Adam's Basin. Soon after our arrival we attended an all-day meeting held by P. A. Smith, an earnest Adventist minister. The First-day Adventists taught that the great commotion among the nations of Europe would bring on the Battle of Armageddon, and the Lord would now come very soon. Under this preaching, my convictions of 1843 were again fully aroused. After meeting, as the minister visited with my brother, he began to talk with me, and obtained a promise from me to serve the Lord. I felt relieved that the way was thus opened for me. I wanted to be in earnest about being a Christian, and as there was to be more meetings in two weeks, I desired the privilege of attending them.

When I looked back to my school, all was dark; I dreaded to think of going back to mix with worldly companions until I had more strength in the truth and evidence of acceptance with the Lord. Then an opportunity came to me to work as a blacksmith apprentice, and learn to iron carriages, intending to enter in business with my brother.

I returned home and told the teacher and my schoolmates I had hired out to become a blacksmith, but did not tell them the main reason why I wanted to leave. They presented before me all the flattering prospects I had aspired after, but this did not move me. My mind was made up to be at my brother's in two weeks to attend the next meeting. I turned away from teachers, friends, and even my own mother, deciding that I must give it all up or be lost. I was longing for truth, light, and pardon.

The truth presented at the meetings shed more light upon the subject of the nearness of the Lord's coming. I began to study the Bible thoroughly. I carried a small pocket Bible to the blacksmith shop and would read it when the rest of the hands were off at a nearby grocery. Sometimes I would retire to a back coal shed and pray. My mind was impressed to speak in public meeting and tell my desires, to pray and ask the prayers of others—a cross I struggled under for several days. When I would pray for the evidence of sins forgiven, it would be impressed upon my mind to be baptized. This troubled me, so I told my brother. He said, "If I felt that way, I would be baptized at the first opportunity. Elder Smith is going to be at Clarkson next Sunday, and is going to baptize one on the way, and you can be baptized at the same time."

When Elder Smith came and I told him of my feelings he said, "Yes, by all means go forward!" I prayed earnestly to the Lord to be guided aright, and went with trembling to the place of baptism. It was a beautiful summer morning, and when I came out of the water I was as happy as I could be. It seemed that all nature praised the Lord. I was now free and could say, I know that the Lord loves me. We had about ten miles to go from there to the meeting, and we sang and praised the Lord all the way.

At the time of my baptism among the First-day Adventists in June 1849, they had no formal organization. They did not keep any record of names. They claimed that on being baptized their names were entered in the "Book of Life" and that was sufficient. If, amid the opposition against the Adventists which raged at that time, one had the courage to publicly accept the faith, they acknowledged them as brethren.

At the shop where I worked, many customers would come in and talk of everything but religion. Whenever they talked with me, I would try to turn the conversation to religious matters, and to the great subject of the near coming of the Lord. Some would listen and seem deeply affected; others would mock and ridicule, but this only made me the stronger. After my day's work was done, I would often sit up until midnight with candle and book by my side to study the truth.

The shop stood close by the Erie Canal, and most of our customers were canal drivers.

Instead of learning anything about carriage work, I was set to pulling horse shoes, clinching nails, filing and finishing the hoofs, etc. During all those three months there was not a wheel carriage in the shop. Since I received no carriage work as promised, I broke off my contract, and received for the three month's work my board and lodging, and a calf-skin leather apron.

Now penniless, I returned to my mother's home in my native village. There I soon began to reap the results of my summer's exposure to the malarial atmosphere on the canal and frog pond. I began chills every alternate day, and soon they came every day, and finally twice a day. After being afflicted this way for two months, I thought my life was doomed.

When the chills began upon me, I was solemnly impressed that it was my duty to go out and preach to others the precious truths I had learned from the Scriptures, but I tried to throw off this conviction with the thought that a boy not yet seventeen was too young to preach. Then again, I had not a penny of money and my clothing was about ready to discard. When the chill was on, it would be vividly impressed upon me to go out and preach, and my chill would stop. So on the day I had two chills in one day, I said, "Lord, break these chills and fever and I will go out and preach as soon as I can recover enough strength to do so." The chills ceased that very day.

After the close of nine weeks of malaria, I was weak physically, but fully determined, as soon as possible, to go out in ministerial work. I hired out to dig a field of potatoes, but had to stop for lack of strength. Then I was given a job of cutting wood. In a few weeks I had saved one dollar above expenses. That would get me where I wanted to go, but what about clothing?

Chapter 3

Teenage Preacher

The neighbor for whom I was working gave me a vest and a pair of trousers, partly worn; but as he was a man much taller than I, these garments, after cutting seven inches off the trousers, were far from being a nice fit. As a substitute for a dress coat, my brother had given me a double-breasted overcoat, the skirt of which had been cut off. With this curious outfit and the $1.00, I decided to go into some area where I was unknown and try to preach. If I failed, my friends would not know it; if I succeeded, I would take that as evidence it was my duty to preach.

One day Caleb Broughton came to me and asked what I thought of doing that winter. I had longed for some way to open to let my feelings be known, but I did not dare say anything for fear I was mistaken. I replied, "I have thought the Lord wanted me to preach, but perhaps I'm mistaken."

"Thank the Lord, Brother John!" he exclaimed. "I've been watching you for a long time, and it seems to me that it is your duty to preach. I'll do anything I can to help you." He then gave me a $3.00 bill, my first gift for such a purpose. This opened the matter to other Adventists, most of whom agreed with the idea of my preaching.

Just after Christmas 1848, I went by train to Rochester, walked 12 miles to Adams Basin, spent the night at my brother's, then walked to Kendall Corners where I knew not a soul in the place. With $5.00 worth of books which had been given me to sell and use the proceeds, I neared the place, lifting my heart to God that He would open the way.

"Can you tell me where any Adventists live in this village?" I asked a man standing beside a house.

"Yes," he replied. "There are Millerites in this house by the name of Thompson."

When I introduced myself as an Adventist preacher, they welcomed me heartily but eyed me curiously. I feared they would ask how long I had been preaching, but they did not. They embarrassed me, however, when they asked me to take off my overcoat, for I had to tell them it was the only coat I had on.

I went to the Baptist preacher and to the trustees of the Baptist church and secured it for three evenings, then gave my appointment for January 2nd, in the school and in the post office. Soon it was going around that a little boy was going to preach.

In the evening I found the church filled to capacity. I sang, prayed, and sang again. I spoke on the subject of the fall of man. Instead of being embarrassed as I feared I would be, the blessing of God came upon me and I spoke freely. The next morning I was told that there were seven ministers present the night before.

The next evening the place was crowded again. I suppose what drew them was curiosity to hear a beardless boy preach, for I was not quite seventeen. At the close of my sermon the Baptist preacher arose and stated that on the next evening a series of singing classes would begin, so my meetings would have to close. Then a Mr. Thompson (son of the man with whom I lodged) stood and said, "Mr. Loughborough, this singing school has been planned for the purpose of closing your meetings. I live in a school district five miles south of here. We have a large schoolhouse, and I am one of the trustees. We have consulted over the matter, and invite you to come and hold meetings there as long as you wish. My house is nearby, and you are welcome to stay with me." I thanked him heartily and said, "Please circulate my appointment to speak in your schoolhouse tomorrow evening."

The next day the Baptist minister called at the home of a family who were interested in my lectures. About a score of neighbors had come in to ask what he thought of the meetings. He replied, "Get that boy to come here and I will use him up in two minutes." So the head of the house sent his boy for me saying, "Come over to our house for dinner right away."

As soon as I was seated in the room where the neighbors had gathered, the door opened from the cabinet shop in the front of the building, and in came the Baptist minister. I had been fearing to meet ministers, so I secretly lifted my heart to God.

The minister began, "Well, you had quite a hearing last evening." "Yes, and they seemed much interested," I said. He replied, "They were probably curious to hear a boy preach, but did I understand you to say last night that the soul is not immortal?" I answered, "I said so. I don't know how you understood me." He then asked, "But what do you do with the text that says 'These go into everlasting punishment, the death that never dies.'?" I was surprised and said, "I don't know of any such scripture. Half of your quotation is in the Bible, and the other half from the Methodist hymnal."

With much earnestness he insisted, "I tell you what I quoted is in the Bible! It's in the 25th chapter of Revelation." I replied, "I guess you mean the 25th chapter of Matthew. Half of your text is there. It says of the wicked that they will go into everlasting punishment." "Oh yes," he agreed. "That's alright, but the text I quoted is in the 25th chapter of Revelation." "Then it is about three chapters outside of the Bible," I said, "for there are only twenty-two chapters in Revelation."

"Let me take your Bible and I will show it to you," he said. To the astonishment of all, he began paging through the Old Testament, then inquired, "Where is Revelation?" I answered, "Look near the last cover of the Bible. It is the last book, but there are only twenty-two chapters in that book." He returned my Bible and said, "Well, I would like to talk with you sometime, but I have another engagement I must meet right now," and in confusion he left the room.

Those present were greatly astonished. One lady commented, "I thought he was a learned man." I explained, "He has a large library and is learned in those books, but he has failed to study his Bible." The family told me that they were much interested in what I preached the night before, and had met there to talk it over, but the minister came and asked them to send for me, and he would show them the fallacy of my teaching. After a good visit with them, I left with my fear of ministers greatly diminished.

After five meetings at Mr. Thompson's schoolhouse, I traveled west to the Twobridge Schoolhouse. Impressed that this would be a good place for meetings, I called at the nearest home. They gave me dinner and showed me where the trustees lived. I saw them and had an appointment given out. The place was filled the first night. Afterwards, a Mr. Beardsley invited me to make my home with him.

With moonlight nights and fine sleighing, I had a packed house every evening. After my ninth lecture, Mr. Beardsley had a charge brought against him of harboring a heretic in his house. He made his defense publicly in one of my meetings, and endorsed what I preached as the truth. This broke the ice and others took their stand. Since the eleven sermons I gave in that place were all I had prepared, I stopped the meetings and went home to rest, and to see to the needs of my widowed mother.

But I still dreaded to go out alone and preach. After a few weeks at home, I started for Mr. Thompson's neighborhood again. On my way I called at Mr. Lamson's at Clarkson, and asked if someone would go with me to help sing and carry on the meetings, but no one could be spared. Finally, Mr. Lamson walked three or four miles with me, carrying my valise and speaking words of encouragement. After we parted, I went a short distance, sat down on my valise by the roadside and wept until I felt relieved. Then I went on and called on my friend Thompson and his family. They were glad to see me and circulated an appointment for that evening.

On arriving at the schoolhouse, we found quite a number of rude fellows with a Universalist school-teacher at their head, who seemed bent upon mischief. When I was there before, they had taken offense at my teaching of immortality alone through Christ, so when I began to preach, they started to whisper, then talk aloud. When I reproved them, they fired at my head a shower of parched corn, shot, and hickory nuts. These did not injure me although they struck with considerable force against the blackboard behind me. Deciding it was useless to proceed further, I closed the meeting. Friend Thompson and others wished me to prosecute the boys, but I objected.

When I reported the incident to Elder Phineas Smith, the minister who baptized me, he invited me to accompany him in meetings at Morganville and Elba. This I did, and it provided excellent schooling for me.

In May, my brother at Adams Basin came down with malaria, and requested me to come and work in his shop. His chills continued most of the summer, so I did not preach but labored with my hands.

In November, I arranged to go with Elder Sullivan Heath, an experienced Adventist minister, and spend the winter in Erie County,

Pennsylvania. So, fitted out with his horse and carriage and a supply of books, we held meetings in Erie, Girard, Washington, and other towns with good results. Friends in Pennsylvania presented me with a horse and light wagon. With this rig I returned in April, and spent the summer in New York.

During 1850, I was afflicted with a slight lung hemorrhage. Since I was advised to use tobacco as a remedy, I began to smoke cigars. But in September 1852, I left off the injurious habit. One day as I lighted a cigar, the filthiness of the tobacco habit passed before me like a panorama in contrast with the character of those who are to dwell in the New Jerusalem. I heard as distinctly as if a voice had spoken, "Suppose the Lord should come and find you with that cigar in your mouth. Would you be permitted into that clean place?" I said to myself, "No! Lord, by thy grace I abandon tobacco forever!" I threw the partly-smoked cigar into the Genesse River, and from that day to this never let a particle of the foul stuff pass my lips. The desire for it completely left me.

In the summer of 1852, I did some house painting in Rochester. When this was over, I found a wife and had to support her. Soon I entered the wholesale and retail trade of Arnold's patent sash locks. It was remunerative labor, and I still filled my Sunday appointments. In the meantime I was studying the subject of the sanctuary and the two-horned beast of Revelation 13. I could find no proof to sustain the First-day Adventist position that the earth was the sanctuary, but I did not discover what the real sanctuary was. While studying Revelation 13, I read in Litch's exposition of the two-horned beast, "I think it is a power yet to be developed as an accomplice of the Papacy in subjecting the world."

I then searched for claims for Sunday-keeping. I decided there was no divine authority for keeping the day holy, so had no misgivings about working on that day. However, I still had the idea that the law as a whole was abolished. Meanwhile some of the leaders among the first-day Adventists dealt dishonestly with me, and partially destroyed my confidence in them.

In midsummer an uncle of mine had a violent attack of fever and chills. He called for me and said, "John, I wish you would read from the fifth chapter of James." I did so. Then he added, "I believe if you will ask Brethren Boughton and Morehouse to join with you in prayer and anoint me with oil, the Lord will heal this fever and I will be well. Will you ask them?" I did so and they immediately came. When we followed the directions in James, he was entirely free from fever, and the room was filled with the presence of the Lord.

A few weeks later I learned that a seventh-day minister had been to Parma, and many Adventists there now believed the United States to be the two-horned beast, and they also had begun to keep the seventh-day Sabbath. Some of the First-day Adventists tried to prejudice my mind against the Sabbath-keepers by saying, "They get together and scream and yell, and have a great noisy fanatical demonstration."

I prayed much about the matter. Then one night I dreamed I sat in an Adventist meeting in Rochester. The room had low, smoky walls and was poorly lighted and ventilated. I recognized in my dream several ministers, among them Joseph Marsh, J. B. Cooke, and O. R. L. Crosier. The people were not only in confusion but looked sad and discouraged. As some of the ministers would arise and preach, their talk seemed to stupefy their listeners. As I meditated upon the situation, a door directly in front of me opened into a much larger room with high walls and a clean, white ceiling. It was well-lighted and ventilated, and everything bore the aspect of good cheer. The people all had Bibles in their hands and seemed to be feasting with great satisfaction on its truths. At the far end of the room hung a chart which differed from any I had ever seen before. It pictured a Jewish Sanctuary, and also the two-horned beast. By the side of the chart stood a tall man whose very countenance indicated earnestness, devotion, and sincerity. In the congregation were brethren from Parma and Hamlin. I dreamed I arose and said, "I'm going to get out of this room and go into the other room." I began to meditate upon the great contrast between the two rooms, and awoke deeply impressed that I would soon

"Yes," said the minister, "but my text is in the twenty-fifth chapter of Revelation."

see great light on the sanctuary and the two-horned beast.

A few days later, Brother Orton of Rochester said to me, "The seventh-day folks are holding meetings at 124 Mt. Hope Ave. Let us go and attend one of their meetings." I replied, "No! I will not go." "But," he argued, "you have a duty there. Some of your flock have joined the Sabbath Adventists, and you ought to get them out of this heresy. They give you a chance to speak in their meeting. Get your texts ready, and you can show them in two minutes that the Sabbath is abolished." So with seven other First-day Adventists, I went to the meeting.

1843 Chart

Chapter 4

Finding the Sabbath Truth

As we went into the room they were in the midst of a testimony meeting. There were no fanatical, boisterous demonstrations, but calm sensible testimonies wet down with tears. Such a heavenly atmosphere greatly impressed me. Then in stepped Harvey Cottrell from Mill Grove, face beaming with the love of God. "Praise the Lord for his goodness to me. I came here last Thursday anxious to attend the meetings, but spent the whole time in bed with fever. At my request the brethren followed the rule in James, anointed me with oil and prayed for me, and I am healed. Praise the Lord." With this quiet, simple statement the Spirit of the Lord filled the room. I said to myself, "That is just as it was in my uncle's case." My prejudice was fast yielding to the conviction that these people had the blessing of the Lord with them.

As I looked about the room I noticed there hung directly in front of me the identical chart I had seen in my dream, and as Elder J. N. Andrews arose to speak, I recognized him, too. He began, "The time announced for the preaching service has come. I had prepared to speak on a certain subject, but during the social meeting my mind turned to another. It may be the Lord's will for me to speak on the texts which are supposed to teach that the Ten Commandments were abolished at the cross." Elder Andrews did not know who I was. No one had said a word to him since I came in.

Beginning with Colossians he took my texts one by one, in the exact order in which I had them marked, and straightened them all out to my perfect satisfaction. In examining Colossians he explained that there are two laws, and the moral law of Ten Commandments is eternal, whereas the law of ceremonies pointed to Christ and ceased at the cross. A solemn impression of the Spirit of God came with his presentation. I said to my-self, "This is the most consistent of anything I have ever heard on the law question. It will settle the whole thing for me." And it did.

In later presentations Elder Andrews covered the subjects of the two-horned beast, the sanctuary and its cleansing, and the three angel's mes-sages. He took pains to make every point clear. Almost daily he visited and prayed with us. The Rochester company did much praying also for the interested ones. It was not simply the bare argument in favor of the truth that so deeply moved us as the evident presence of the Spirit which ac-companied the presentation of those truths, and broke the fallow ground in our hearts. I could not keep away from the meetings nor resist the pow-erful arguments presented.

When I accepted the Sabbath truth in September 1852, I still had ap-pointments for three Sundays for the First-day Adventists. I decided to fill these appointments, but say nothing concerning the new light, for I knew I must be well prepared to defend my position. At each place I told them I would come no more.

My fourth Sabbath was spent in Rochester. On that day I publicly took my stand with this people for the third angel's message, and handed in an article for the *Review* announcing my change of faith. In the meet-ing that day I first saw Elder and Mrs. White. They had been away from Rochester for about three months, traveling by horse and carriage visiting scattered Sabbath-keepers in New England.

This Sabbath meeting was held at 124 Mt. Hope Avenue. The room for religious purposes, place of residence, and printing office of the *Review and Herald* were all in the same building, and Oswald Stowell was the pressman. At this time he had been suffering very severe attacks of pleurisy and had been given up by the physicians to die. Stowell was in the adjoining room and at the close of the Sabbath service sent in a request for prayer.

After I was introduced to the Whites, they invited me to go in with them for a season of prayer while the rest of the company remained in silent prayer in the meeting room. We bowed by the bedside, and while prayer was being offered, Elder White anointed Brother Stowell in the name of the Lord and he was instantly healed. When we arose from prayer, he was sitting up striking his sides which before had been so painful. "I am fully healed and shall be able to work tomorrow," he said. The same blessing that healed him fell in still greater measure upon Sister White. As Elder White turned to look he said, "Ellen is in vision. She does not breathe while in this condition. If any of you desire to satisfy yourselves of this fact, you are at liberty to examine her."

She was kneeling beside the bed with her eyes open in a far-away look as if gazing intently at some object, not in a vacant stare but in a pleasant, intelligent expression. Her countenance appeared fresh and florid. Though she looked upward, her head would turn from side to side as she seemed to be viewing different objects. It was evident from many tests applied that she was entirely oblivious to anything transpiring around her. Her hands would move gracefully from time to time. She remained in vision half an hour or more. While in that condition she spoke words and sometimes distinct sentences; yet by the closest scrutiny, no breath could be discerned in her body. When she came out of vision her first three breaths were like that of a newborn child's first breath.

After she came out of vision, she bore a testimony for that company there assembled. She spoke to me especially, delineating the working of my mind before embracing the truth, even of thoughts which I had expressed to no one. As I heard these things from her lips, I said, "Surely there is a power more than human connected with this vision."

There were eight of us First-day Adventists who accepted the truth under the labors of Elder J. N. Andrews in Rochester. Before the Whites returned from the Eastern tour, one of these persons left the city and traveled on business in Michigan. In relating her vision, Mrs. White told us that she saw a man who, while traveling away from home, had much to say about the law of God and the Sabbath, yet at the same time was breaking one of those commandments. She said he was a person she had never met, yet she believed she would see him sometime since his case had been unfolded to her. Not one of our company, however, supposed it to be anyone we knew.

About six weeks later, the aforementioned brother returned from Michigan. As soon as Sister White saw him, she said, "This is the man I saw in vision of which I told you." Sister White related to this man in the presence of his wife and several other persons what she was shown, then said, "As Nathan said to David, Thou art the man."

After listening to Mrs. White's rehearsal of his wrong doing, he dropped upon his knees before his wife and with tears said, "God is with you of a truth." Then he made a full confession of how he had been trapped into violation of the seventh commandment at Paw Paw, Michigan, over 500 miles from Rochester. He said this was the first offense of that kind in his life and it would be his last.

For three and one-half years I had preached for the First-day Adventists, but supported myself principally by my own labor. When I accepted the truth I had about $35 in hand. I still made earnest efforts to push the windowlock business in which I had been successful. Now as I went from place to place with the business, the conviction constantly pressed upon me to make known to others the truths I had learned. With all the efforts I put forth, my business would not prosper. Sometimes my sales for a week would only pay my fare and hotel bill. This state of things soon consumed what money I had saved, leaving me without money to pay my fare out of Rochester. Finally, about mid-December, my money was reduced to a silver three-cent piece.

A cloud seemed to hang over the next Sabbath meeting I attended. As prayer was offered for the removal of the cloud, Sister White was taken off in vision. On relating the vision she had a message for me: "The reason this cloud hangs over the meeting is that Brother Loughborough is resisting the conviction of duty. God wants him to give himself wholly to the preaching of the message."

I did not take my stand then to do it for I could not see how I could be supported in so doing. On reaching home, I told the Lord if He would open the way I would go out; but this did not settle it. Finally, on the strength of the testimony I said, "I will obey, Lord, and Thou wilt open the way." At once all those perplexing doubts passed from my mind and I was happy in the thought that the Lord would provide.

On the following Monday morning my wife, who did not know how low our funds were, came to ask for money with which to buy matches and some thread. Taking the money from my pocket I said, "Mary, here is a three-cent piece. It's all the money I have in the world. Get only one cent's worth of matches, spend only one of the other cents, and bring me one cent so we will not be entirely out of money. I have tried hard, every way in my power to make my business succeed, but I cannot."

With tears she asked, "John, what in the world are we going to do?"

I replied, "I have been powerfully convicted for weeks that the reason my business does not succeed is because the Lord's hand is against it for neglect of duty. It is my duty to give myself wholly to the preaching of the truth."

"But," she objected, "if you go to preach, how are we to be supported?"

I answered, "As soon as I decided to obey the call of duty, there came to me the assurance that the Lord is going to open the way. I don't know how it will be done, but the way will open."

She retired to her room to weep and perhaps to pray; at least I saw no more of her for an hour. Then as she went out to make her little purchases I pitied her sad heart. No more than thirty minutes later there was a loud rap at the door. A gentleman inquired for me and I let him in. After introducing himself he said, "Because of my poor health I am moving to Ohio, and I wish to take along some small business with which to meet expenses. Mr. Garbutt recommended you as being able to purchase Arnold's patent sash-locks. I want an assortment of eighty dollars' worth and will pick them up tomorrow noon and pay you the money."

Now all I would have to do would be to walk half a mile to the factory and leave the order. They would bring the locks to my door and I would receive the commission of $26 which had much purchasing power in those days.

Soon after the man left, my wife returned and found me singing. "You seem happy," she commented. "Yes," I agreed. "While you were at the store I had company. The Lord has opened the way for me to go out and preach the message." When I told her of the order for the locks, with a flood of different tears she retired to her room to weep and seek the Lord. Soon she returned as happy as I and ready to do what she could to prepare me for my labors. On receiving the money, I purchased wood, provisions, and whatever necessary home comforts should I enter the field.

On the next Sabbath (*December* 18) there was a general gathering of Sabbath-keepers of western New York, and during the prayer Sister White was taken off in vision. Among other things presented to her was a message for me. "You are correct in your decision to give yourself to the work of the ministry. It is now your duty to go, and tarry no longer." Prayer was then offered that the Lord would further open my way.

Hiram Edson, who lived forty miles east of Rochester, had decided not to attend the meeting, but his wife was so impressed that he would be called away that she readied his clothing for any emergency. On Sabbath, *December* 16, while conducting family worship, the impression came to him, "Go to Rochester. You are wanted there." He asked his wife, "What does this mean? I don't know why I should go to Rochester."

Several times during the day when he went to the barn to pray, the impression would come, "Go to Rochester." Finally, he asked his wife, "Is my clothing in condition to leave? I feel that I may be gone for several weeks." She assured him that all was ready. After the close of the Sabbath, he took the train to Rochester. On arriving he said to Elder White, "I hadn't planned to come to this meeting, but I have been strongly impressed today that I should come, and here I am. What do you want with me?"

"Well," said Elder White, "we want you to take old Charlie horse and the carriage, and take Brother Loughborough around on a six-weeks circuit in southwestern New York and get him started preaching the message." So the following Monday, Brother Edson and I started out with Elder White's horse and carriage for a six-week trip.

Chapter 5

"Very Bad Injun"

Traveling to Orangeport, we spent our first Sabbath with a company of believers there. A heavy snowstorm made it impossible to go any farther with the carriage, so on Sunday we constructed a four-runner sleigh, or "pung," and went on our way.

On Christmas Eve 1852, we drove into Buffalo in a terrible snowstorm. Up to this time I had never owned an overcoat, so Brother Edson stopped at a clothing store and bought me one. We then drove on to Fredonia and held meetings for a few days. From there we went to Potter County, Pennsylvania, visiting scattered ones along the way.

At State Line, Lewis Hacket had arranged for me to speak Sunday afternoon and evening in a large schoolhouse. Since the forenoon was already taken by another minister, we decided to attend and further circulate our appointment. When the minister failed to appear, the congregation asked me to speak. As I stepped to the desk, the people gave me a very curious look, but soon began to show deep interest. In the afternoon and evening the place was packed to utmost capacity.

As I went into Mr. Hacket's shoe-shop on Monday morning, I noticed a copy of the handbill with which he had notified the town of my meetings. This explained the peculiar looks of the people the day before. It read, "J. N. Loughborough of Rochester will speak at the schoolhouse at two and seven p.m. Come and hear, for they which have turned the world upside down are come hither also, whom Lewis hath received. And these do all contrary to the pope's decrees, saying there is a better way—the commandments of God and the faith of Jesus." I asked, "Is this the way you notified the town? Now I can understand why the people gave me such a curious look when I first stood before them."

As we started our homeward trip down the Genesee River to Rochester, we had to hurry for the snow was melting fast. We stopped over Sabbath with a family of believers. The husband in the family seemed very anxious to preach the message, but we gave him no encouragement for we felt he took life altogether too easy to make a success of preaching. We noticed that his wife was out cutting wood to prepare his supper while he sat in an easy chair, his feet upon another, and sang with enthusiasm about the easy time he expected in heaven. One stanza delighted him most, "We'll have nothing at all to do but march around Jerusalem, when we arrive at home." He seemed to illustrate the spirit of his song by having nothing to do with labor and toil on earth.

When we reached Attica, New York, the snow had all melted off the road, so we had to walk to relieve the horse in drawing our pung over the bare ground. We reached Rochester in good health and good cheer after an absence of six weeks. But now, as Hiram Edson returned to his home, I had to ride on the back of old Charlie with the harness some fifty miles to Orangeport to get the carriage we left there in December.

During the winter of 1852–53, into the Rochester company came a man who was loud and boisterous in his testimony. He said, "There's a position we can reach where we shall have no more temptations." It sounded a bit strange to me, and judging by the look of Elder and Mrs. White, I did not think they endorsed his theology either.

The next Sabbath the man exhorted us to come upon higher ground where we would be free from temptation. The climax came the third Sabbath. This zealous one bellowed, "Brethren, come up on the platform where I am. COME UP! COME UP!

Rising to his feet Elder White very calmly said to the man, "You speak of being upon some platform. It reminds me of a man of small stature in Christ's time who wanted to see the Saviour and climbed into a sycamore tree. When the Saviour came along, He said, 'Zaccheus, make haste and come down.' I will now say to you, Zaccheus, come down. If there is a place where we will not be tempted anymore, let us know how to get there. With irony I tell you that you have sat down on the easy stool of the devil when you think that all your impressions are from the Lord, and you will be led into gross sins."

The man protested that it would not be so, yet six weeks later he came into his house with a woman much younger than his wife clinging to his arm. As he entered the room, he said to his wife who was holding her two-month-old babe, "Thus saith the Lord, Cast out the bondwoman and her son, for the son of the bondwoman shall not be heir with the son of the freewoman." He then invited his wife to leave, giving her to understand that the woman on his arm was now the mistress of the house. As his wife did not propose to walk the cold, wintry streets with a babe in her arms, she refused to go. Shortly afterwards, the man had a case to settle with the civil authorities. This ended all his profession of the third angel's message.

During the winter of 1852–53, Elder Andrews wrote his 80-page pamphlet on the sanctuary and 2,300 days. This was printed on the hand press in the spring of 1853. The office had no stitching or trimming machine. Elder White, anxious to send copies to all the brethren, called a "bee" of the Rochester members who folded the signatures for 100 books. I perforated them with a shoemaker's pegging awl, the sisters stitched them with needle and thread, Mary Patten put on the covers, and Uriah Smith trimmed them with his pocket knife and straight edge. Sister White wrapped them, and Elder White addressed them for the mail. We were a happy company together for we were getting off the first book printed on a press owned by Seventh-day Adventists.

In the early years of my ministry, I had labored together with Elder Sullivan Heath, a First-day Adventist who shortly afterwards moved to Illinois. His relatives in Clarkson, New York had accepted present truth and, anxious that he hear also, raised money for my expenses to visit him. Elder White suggested that instead of simply going to Illinois and back, I should visit the few at Fredonia, New York and Milan, Ohio, and some points in Michigan, then meet them at Jackson on June 21. So I left in May with this intention.

In 1853, the plan was adopted of giving the ministers a card recommending them to fellowship with our people everywhere. The one given me in January, 1853, reads: "Brother Loughborough of Rochester, New York is one whom we recommend to the brethren where he may travel."

In behalf of the church, (signed) James White
Joseph Bates, leading ministers.

After passing through Ohio, I went on to Michigan and met Elder Cornell at his house in Plymouth. We went together to Tyrone, Locke, and Jackson. Here we parted, he to meet the Whites at Tyrone, and I to go to Battle Creek, Bedford, and Hastings, then to return and meet him at Jackson. Here a very striking incident occurred.

When I reached the home of Cyrenius Smith in Jackson, the Whites and the Cornells were there. Elder Cornell met me at the door and took me to a grove near the house before I saw Elder or Mrs. White. He told me that Sister White had had a vision, and gave me all the particulars. He said she had written it out and hoped I would get a copy of it, for part of it was about a corrupt woman they knew, and she had given an exact description of the case. Elder and Mrs. White had an appointment where this woman lived, but they themselves did not know where she lived. Sister White kept asking him if he knew, but he would evade a definite answer, telling them that if there were such a woman in the state they would probably find her. I agreed with Elder Cornell to say nothing to them about it, but would try to obtain a copy of the vision, and we would watch to see how the thing came out.

When I went into the house, Sister White began at once to tell me of the wonderful meeting they had at Tyrone in which the Lord had given her a vision of all the Sabbath-keepers in the state, and among other things about a woman who claimed to be so holy she did not need the Ten Commandments, but who was represented to her as a corrupt woman. She continued, "I have been writing out this vision and will read it to you." She had written with pencil upon eight pages of foolscap.

I said, "Sister White, I would like a copy of that vision."

She replied, "This is written with pencil, but if you will make a copy with ink for me, you may have the pencil copy."

The copy of the vision described the case of a woman professing great holiness, and who was trying to intrude herself among our people. Mrs.

White had never met her, and had no knowledge of her except what was imparted in vision. She not only told the woman's mode of procedure but also that when she should be reproved, she would put von a sanctimonious look and say, "The - Lord - knows - my - heart." She said this woman was traveling about the country with a young man, while her own husband, an old man, worked at home to support them in their evil course.

After we had meetings in Battle Creek and Hastings, we drove to Vergennes, arriving about four o'clock in the afternoon. We called first on a former Christian minister who lived in a log house yet three miles from the place where the meetings were to be held the next day. Elders White, Cornell, and I stopped under a large apple tree in the yard while Sister White went into the house and talked about the day's journey. Soon she came out and said to her husband, "James, we have reached the church where that woman lives."

"How do you know?" he asked.

She replied, "I have seen the man and woman in this house in vision. He thinks the (corrupt) woman is all right, but she thinks the woman is wrong."

Elder Cornell, who knew the people, whispered to me, "She is absolutely right!!"

When someone announced, "Brother Brigham is coming," Mrs. White looked up and said, "I saw them also in connection with this case, but none in that load have any confidence in the woman." When the next load drove up she said, "That load is divided on the woman's case.

Those on the front seat have no confidence, but those in the back think she is all right."

A third load came up and she said of them, "They are all under the woman's influence." Then she added. "There is one man who is opposed to this woman whom I have not yet seen. He has sandy hair and a sandy beard, and there's something peculiar about his eyes."

Just then someone remarked, "Brother Pearsall is coming." "Oh," she said, "that is the man who has spectacles on." There was indeed something peculiar about his eyes. As I was talking with him, I commented about his wearing glasses when he was so young. He explained that his eyes were not mates; one was nearsighted and the other farsighted, so he had special glasses made for him. Elder Cornell and I were where we could whisper occasionally unobserved, and he told me he was acquainted with all these people and the positions they took, and that Mrs. White had declared their positions exactly.

We had no meeting that night. The next morning we went another three miles to the place of meeting. The brethren had made ample provision by seating a large barn, but they had made no stand for the speakers, so we took a new wagon box and turned it upside down to serve as a rostrum. A common light stand was placed on one end of the box, and chairs were used for seats. Sister White sat in a rocking chair at the left end of the rostrum, and I sat next to her with Elder Cornell on my right. Elder White stood preaching at the far end. After he had been speaking about ten minutes, a tall, slim, dark-complexioned woman entered and sat next to the door, followed by an old gentleman and a young man who sat down on the front seat within touch of the stand. I noticed that Mrs. White looked intently at these people. She put her fan to her face and whispered to me, "Do you see the tall woman who just sat down by the door? She is the woman I saw in vision. That old man who sat down in front is her husband, and the young man in the green coat beside him is the one with whom the woman is going about the country. When James gets through, I shall relate the vision and you will see whether or not they are the ones." I confess I was anxious to see how things would develop for I had in writing in my pocket just what this woman would say when Sister White would reprove her.

After a short message, Elder White turned to his wife, "I think someone else has something to say and I will close."

Mrs. White introduced her remarks with the text, "Be ye clean that bear the vessels of the Lord." Finally she said, "If the Lord called a woman to the ministry, she would not be traveling about the country with a man other than her husband." On uttering these words, there was much agitation in the audience, some nudging their seatmates, and whispering, "Just as I told you."

Sister White came still closer, "Friends, what I am talking about is right here before us. That tall woman who came in and sat by the door a few moments ago claims to be very holy. She also claims to have the gift of tongues. The words she rattles off are mere gibberish. If every nation on earth heard her, not one of them could understand a thing for she does not talk any language. This woman claims a holiness so high she does not need the Ten Commandments. She professes to be sanctified. This old man on the front seat is her husband. God pity him. He toils at home to earn money for her to travel around the country with this young man who sits by his side—supporting them in their iniquity. God has shown me that with all their pretensions to holiness, this woman and this young man are guilty of violating the seventh commandment."

After a few more words, Sister White sat down. The people knew that Mrs. White had just come three miles from her lodging place, and that the other woman had come two miles from the opposite direction, and they had not seen each other before.

As Mrs. White bore her testimony there was an anxious looking toward Mrs. Alcott, the woman reproved, to see how she took it. Had she been innocent of the charge, it would naturally be expected for her to deny the whole thing. With every eye fixed upon her, she slowly rose to her feet, and with a sanctimonious look said slowly, "The - Lord - knows - my - heart," and sat down. Then the forenoon meeting closed.

After we left the barn to take dinner at a brother's house nearby, the woman rallied the people together for a prayer meeting. It was a complete bedlam of voices calling at once, "O Lord! O Lord!" She asked the young man to pray, and what a prayer it was! "O Lord, take care of our persecutors. Send a bucket of tar and a bag of feathers, and a wooden horse, and ride them out of town on a rail," and many other expressions of similar character. Then for a few minutes Mrs. Alcott talked, making no reference whatever to Sister White's talk, but went on to teach her doctrine of sanctification. In the midst of this she broke out with what she called tongues. I reached the barn in time to hear, "Kenne kenni, kenne kenno, kenne kenne, kenne kennue," and the same combined in other order. Then her meeting closed.

It was a hot summer day, and we were taking dinner in a small room. The people pressed so thickly about, stifling the air, that Sister White fainted. Elder White and I offered prayer. The blessing of God came, restoring consciousness, but she was immediately off in vision. Elder White took her up in his arms and carried her out-of-doors among the people who were anxious to see her in vision. Our meeting for the remainder of the day was instruction upon the truths for our people.

The sequel I now relate was told me by residents of Vergennes who carefully watched the case. The next Sunday after our meeting, Mrs. Alcott held a meeting at the school-house. A curious crowd came to hear what she would now say. She made no reference to Sister White, but went on a harangue about holiness. She claimed that she and the young man were being prepared to enter upon a mission among the Highland Indians who lived a few miles away. While she was talking, an Indian lad from the reservation passed the house with his gun on the way to a hunt.

Some of the boys who sat near the door asked him to come in for the woman could talk his language. They gave him a seat near the door. As soon as Mrs. Alcott saw him, she broke out with her "Kenne kenni." The Indian stared at her for a while, then seizing his gun he gave a whoop and started off on a run. The boys ran after him and asked what the woman had said. He replied, "Very bad injun that!" "But what did she say?" they pressed him. He replied, "Nothing. She talk no Injun!"

A son of Mr. Alcott by a previous marriage went to his father's house and told this woman what he thought of her. He said, "If God has called you on a mission to the Indians, why are you not about it? I don't believe you can talk the language of the tribe. Will you go with me to the interpreter's house and talk and have it tested?" She agreed and he took her to the interpreter. "Here is a woman who talks your language. I want you to tell me what she says."

After she had talked in tongues and prayed in tongues the interpreter said, "Madam, I have been interpreter for seventeen different tribes of Indians, and you have not uttered a single Indian word." This ended her influence in Vergennes. Shortly before leaving town, the young man friend admitted, "What Mrs. White said about us is all true—too true!"

Chapter 6

Western Itinerary

The Sabbath following the Vergennes meeting, Elder Cornell and I met with the little company at Grand Rapids. We were told that a steamer crossed Lake Michigan from Grand River to Milwaukee, Wisconsin, so we planned to cross, taking our horse and carriage, and labor among the scattered brethren in the West.

On Monday we started for the mouth of the Grand River on the Lake Michigan shore.

Thinking to make the distance in half a day, we did not take much food, but to our dismay we had a forty-mile drive. After eating our meager lunch we became hungry by two o'clock. While passing through a grove of pine trees, we came upon a half-acre thickly covered with wintergreen plants. What a sight of berries we could pluck by the handful! This find well supplied our lack of food.

Toward evening we stopped at a hotel by the lakeside and there learned that the steamer did not run to Milwaukee but to Chicago. We made the trip in about twenty hours, landing on the west side of the Chicago River on Wednesday in mud a foot deep. Our fine horse had been terrified all the way across due to the noise of the steam and machinery, and would neither eat nor drink while on the boat. After pulling us and the carriage a half-mile through the mud, he was able to rest on higher ground and feed on prairie grass while we replanned our tour.

The nearest point of meeting any of our people was Alden, two days journey from Chicago. On Friday, the day we were to reach Brother Chapman's in Alden, as we turned aside to feed our horse, stretched before us was a great mass of large, ripe, wild strawberries. We filled our 12-quart water bucket with berries, then pulled them up by the stems, tying up large clusters. This was a feast for us and the Chapmans for the three days we were at their home.

Elder Cornell and I had the names of the persons in Wisconsin who were keeping the Sabbath and reading the *Review*, and it was our purpose to call upon them all. On the next Sabbath we visited Brother and Sister Brown in Beloit, and the following Sabbath met with the few believers in Madison at the home of Brother Turner. Though the number was small we held meetings and had an interesting time. About all the reading matter we had for our people at that time was the eight-page *Review* every two weeks, the monthly Youth's Instructor, a few pamphlets and Mrs. White's Experience & Views.

After visits with other isolated believers, we came to Koshkonong where there was a company of twenty, the largest number of any one place in the state. We had the name of the most prominent one among them, and as we neared the settlement we inquired for him. Finally we saw a man in a cornfield near the road. Elder Cornell said, "I am going to ask that man the question asked in the Apocrypha of the Old Testament."

First he inquired for the home of Milton Southwick. The man said, "He lives in the second house from here." Elder Cornell then asked, "Has righteousness that maketh a man righteous been through this land?"

"Yes!" the man replied. "There are a few of us here who are trying to keep all the Commandments of God. Are you not the brethren from the East of whom we read in the *Review* who are coming to Wisconsin?"

The man was Elder Phelps, leader of their company. Here we spent several days speaking to them and neighbors who ventured in. On learning we would come back that way on our trip to Illinois, they promised to seat a grove for a meeting on our return.

We were especially anxious to meet J. H. Waggoner, former editor of a county paper, who had accepted the truth and begun to preach. He had been active among the Baptists. He lived at Packwaukee, a day's journey farther north. When we reached there we learned he was holding a series of meetings another day's journey to the west. T. M. Steward of Packwaukee, who had begun to keep the Sabbath, piloted us with his horse and carriage to the place of Waggoner's labors. When we arrived, we found him suffering with granulated eyelids, and so we filled his appointments for him.

Then we went still farther north to Metomen to meet J. M. Stephenson and D. P. Hall, two active First-day Adventist ministers who had just taken their stand for the Sabbath. We held a week's meetings so that they might be more fully instructed in the truth.

From this point we began our journey south with Waggoner, Stephenson, and Hall accompanying us as far as Koshkonong. About half-way there lived a devoted brother and his wife who were anxious that their town have opportunity to hear "The United States in Prophecy." The men accompanying us had no faith we would have a congregation and voted that I should speak. To our surprise the schoolhouse was packed. As we journeyed on the next day, these brethren complained that I had taken all the time and not given them a chance to speak.

After the grove meeting at Koshkonong, Stephenson and Hall returned home, and Elder Cornell and I expected to go that night to the home of Stephen Bragg, some 12 miles over an unfamiliar road. A brother who lived only a mile off the road had a request from his ten-year-old son who was suffering from a severe fever, that we stop and have prayer for him. The man said, "My boy says that if you will come and pray for him, he will be well." We told the man we did not see how we could turn off the road that distance and still reach Brother Bragg's before dark. After we started out on what we supposed to be the right road, we found our way blocked by a gate, and the brother's house just inside the gate. He rushed out and exclaimed, "We are so glad you decided to come!" The facts were we were so busy talking, the horse had taken the wrong road. We had prayers for the boy, and just as his faith had claimed, he was instantly healed of his fever. We were able to complete our journey before dark.

Brother Chapman at Alden had seated a grove near his house for a two-day meeting and had thoroughly advertised. The Seventh-day Baptist minister of Big Foot Prairie canceled his appointments and brought his whole church for the meetings.

At that time the country was open prairie, and no fenced roads, so we had to keep our course to Shabbona Grove sixty miles farther south by sighting some distant object, then making for that object. After spending two days here with a devoted couple, we journeyed to Sullivan Heath's at Barron Grove where we held meetings in a shed between two cribs of corn. With our charts hung upon the cribs we instructed the Heath family as though we had a large audience.

Then we went on to Brother Lock's at Salem, Indiana, where they prepared a grove for meetings which were well attended. Just before sundown on Sunday, we baptized eight souls. After the congregation separated and I was about to change clothing, Brother Bodly requested, "I can't have you brethren leave without taking my stand. Will you go back in the stream and baptize me?" I consented, and in the shades of the evening baptized this earnest soul. The Lord greatly blessed us as we stood alone in the stream.

From Indiana, Elder Cornell and I continued on to Plymouth, Michigan. Toward the last of the trip, as I stepped from the carriage, I hit the first finger of my left hand hard against the tire of the wheel, which resulted in a severe infection. When we reached Plymouth that finger was as large as three, and my arm swollen to the shoulder. In such misery I could not sleep nights. At Plymouth I received a letter from my wife stating that she and Drusilla Orton had been visiting the Woodhulls with whom they were formerly acquainted in Rochester, and they were anxious for me to stop at their home in Olcott, New York They met me at Lockport and I returned with them. They wished a meeting in Olcott at once. I explained, "With this terrible infection I have not slept for two nights."

Sister Woodhull said, "Give out the appointment. We will pray and the Lord will heal you." This was done, and sure enough, all the pain ceased, the swelling subsided, and the core came out of the boil before time for the next evening's appointment.

My wife and Mrs. Orton had faithfully presented the truth to the Woodhull family but they had not made a decision to obey. One morning Mrs. Woodhull asked them, "If this is all true that you've been telling me, and is really the last message, why is there not someone having visions as Joel's prophecy mentions?"

All we had of Sister White's writings then was Experiences and Views. They handed her a copy saying, "Sister Woodhull, we will do your work while you read this."

She sat in another room and read while they worked. She would read and sigh and wipe tears from her eyes. She said not a word until she had completed the book.

"That settles it!" she exclaimed. "I am satisfied now. I shall keep the Sabbath." They remained faithful the rest of their lives and both lived to be over seventy years of age.

Since the Michigan believers wished me to live and labor in their state, we left New York on November 1, with a stop-over at Milan, Ohio. But such interest was awakened in Huron and Seneca counties, we could not leave Ohio until May, 1854.

On May 18 and 19 we held meetings in a schoolhouse at Locke, Michigan. Such a crowd came that two schoolhouses that size could not have held them. In the emergency we took out a window and improvised a pulpit in the empty space so we could speak to all the people, inside and outside, seated in their carriages and on the grass.

The sight of this large assembly led to conversation the next day as to the feasibility of holding tent meetings. As we traveled to Sylvan, Elder White suggested that by another year we might venture the use of a tent. "Why not have one at once?" Elder Cornell urged. The more we talked the more we were impressed to do so.

On arriving at C. S. Glover's about noon on the 22nd, Elder White explained to him what we thought of doing. He asked what the tent would cost. When he was told that $200 would deliver it to Jackson, he handed Elder White $35 saying, "This is what I think of it."

By late afternoon we reached Jackson and saw Brethren Smith, Palmer, and J. P. Kellogg. Each of these expressed his opinion in the same manner as had Brother Glover, with the exception of Brother Kellogg who promised to lend us all that was lacking to purchase it. Near sunset of that day, Elders White, Cornell and I retired to a grove and laid the matter before the Lord in earnest prayer. At noon of May 23, Elder Cornell started for Rochester to purchase of E. C. Williams the first meeting tent ever used by Seventh-day Adventists.

In the evening of the same day, Elder White and his wife were to take the train for Wisconsin. After seeing Elder Cornell off on his train, we spent the afternoon at D. R. Palmer's near the railroad station. As it neared the time to take the train, Elder White began to pace the floor in a solemn mood. "I feel strangely about this trip," he remarked. "If we had not made an appointment, I would not take the train." He asked that we have a season of prayer for their safety. When we arose from prayer, Elder White said, "We will go trusting in the Lord."

At 9 p.m. I went onto the train with them to assist with their hand luggage. We went into a car with high-back seats, called in those days a "sleeping car." Mrs. White hesitated, "James, I cannot stay in this car." But these were the seats she usually preferred. I then assisted in getting them into the last car on the train." As Sister White took her seat she remarked, "I do not feel right on this train." She did not even put up her handbag in the rack for such parcels. The car bell rang, and I bade them goodbye and went to spend the night at Smith's in West Jackson.

About ten o'clock we were all much surprised to hear Elder White, whom we supposed was well on the way to Chicago, knocking for admittance. He told us the train had run off the track three miles west of Jackson; that most of the train was a total wreck, but while a number had been killed, he and his wife had escaped injury. He soon secured a horse and carriage, and in company with Abram Dodge, went for Mrs. White who he had previously carried across a marsh to a place of safety.

Early the next morning I went with Mr. Dodge to view the wreck. At a point where the road crossed the track obliquely, an ox had lain down directly on the track. The engine had no cow-catcher, and was thrown from the track. The baggage car, containing Elder White's trunk of books, jumped entirely clear from the tracks undamaged. At the same time, the passenger car at the rear of the train was uncoupled without human aid and stopped on the track. As we viewed the wreck, we felt in our hearts that God sent His angel to uncouple the car. The brakeman said he did not uncouple it, that no one was on the platform when it occurred, and that it was a mystery to all the trainmen. Even more mysterious to them, the link and the bolt were both unbroken, and the bolt with its chain was lying on the platform of the wrecked car as though placed there by a careful hand. By the evening of the 24th, the track was cleared and the Whites made a safe passage to their Wisconsin appointments.

Chapter 7

Our First Tent Meetings

At Rochester, Elder Cornell went directly to the sail loft of E. C. Williams. Pleased to learn that we were going to use tents in our labors, this earnest First-day Adventist said, "I have a ten-ounce circular tent 60 feet in diameter which was used only 10 days on a state fairground. It is as good as new. Since I got a good price for the use of it, I will sell it to you for the cost of the material—$160. In addition I will give you a nice bunting flag 15 ft. in length with the motto on it 'What is Truth?' "The bargain was speedily completed and in a few hours the tent was on its way to Jackson.

In two weeks from the time we first spoke of the tent enterprise, our tent was erected in Battle Creek on the southeast corner of Tompkins and Van Buren Streets. It was my privilege to give the first sermon. Our voices sounded well from that elevated location. They said they could hear me preach a mile away. Elder Cornell spoke alternately with me in that meeting.

Mr. Noble, the postmaster of Battle Creek, lived not far from the tent and became very interested. He told everyone he saw to go up to the tent and they would hear something worthwhile. So we had crowds in those three days of our first tent-meetings by Seventh-day Adventists.

Returning from Wisconsin about the middle of June, the Whites met with us at Grand Rapids for a three-day general meeting of our people in that part of the state. It also gave the crowd of citizens at our meeting an opportunity to learn our beliefs.

After taking down the tent, a meeting for prayer and counsel was held in the home of one of our brethren. During that meeting I was ordained to the gospel ministry by prayer and laying on of hands of Elders White and Cornell, the first service of this kind among Seventh-day Adventists.

Over the Fourth of July we held meetings at Tyrone near the home of Elder Cornell's father. Then our next meeting was in a grove about three miles from Rochester, Michigan Since this was in the midst of haying and harvest, we would pitch our tent on Friday afternoon, and have two meetings on Sabbath and three on Sunday. Then we would roll up our canvas and work four and a half days for wages with which to meet our tent expenses and care for our families.

Prior to this time, no effort had been made to sell our tracts and pamphlets to the public. They were given away to those interested, and the expenses met by donations from our people. When Elder White suggested that people might be willing to pay a small price for them and thus enable us to publish more, I promised to try it. So on Sundays of a series of meetings we offered books for sale, displaying them on the speaker's stand before us.

At 9 a.m. the third Sunday of the tent-meeting, the grove was full of people. Our tent was full and enough seated on the ground to fill another tent of the same size. Our tent-master counted 246 wagonloads of people who had come on the grounds besides those on foot and on horseback, an estimated 2,000 persons. We invited Elder Russell, a Methodist minister, to give his views on the Sabbath question at 10.30 a.m. I had the sermon on the perpetuity of the law at 9 a.m. which Elder Russel heard. He had his sermon written down, but in reading it he would sometimes turn two or three leaves at a time. Some in the audience said afterwards that my sermon had spoiled his manuscript. His talk was actually a confirmation of what had been said before, - that the foundation for Sunday-keeping lies in tradition with no command from scripture.

At the close of the elder's talk, we announced an examination of his sermon at one o'clock and requested him especially to remain. He declined, even with the most earnest entreaties of his members. Our congregation all remained as they had come prepared to spend the day. After the last meeting the people bought the few books we had for sale: $50 worth.

For $0.35 they could buy a full set of all we had to offer. Some also placed expense money on the stand, amounting to $18.

Among those in our audience on this last day of our meeting was R. J. Lawerence, an earnest Baptist minister. As he rode home on his horse, his neighbors who had been attending asked him what he thought of the day's talk. Putting his hand to his head, he replied, "O, my head is so full I shall have to take three days to think it out." As a result of his thinking he became a Seventh-day Adventist minister, and spent the rest of his life in this cause.

In our first season's effort with the tent we had meetings in eleven places. We called this "running the tent." It might have indeed been considered running from place to place were it not that though each effort was comparatively short, a full condensed line of truth was given to the people, and some souls accepted. We were hurrying on with the idea of awakening an interest in many places to be followed up afterwards.

Our winter labors of 1854–55 were in the state of New York. When our people there learned of the tent effort success in Michigan, they purchased a tent and wagon for New York. They also bought and presented to me the horse and carriage formerly used in the travels of Elder and Mrs. White. A sixty-foot tent was purchased on the last of May, 1855, and erected in the dooryard of Harvey Cottrell of Mill Grove. Here, with R. F. Cottrell for tentmaster, our summer efforts began.

On July 4 while Brother Cottrell and I were traveling with the tent from Mannsville to West Winfield, we had to cross Salmon Creek. Since the bridge had been carried away by a spring freshet, the stream had to be forded. A heavy rain the night before had swollen the waters more than we realized. It was a rapid stream with rocky bottom and did not look deep. Our fording place was between a foot-bridge and a mill-pond. As we came up to it we saw no fresh tracks, so we asked a family living nearby if any teams had passed through. "Oh, yes," a woman replied.

Brother Cottrell walked over the foot-bridge, but as I drove into the water it came up to the wagon bed and over the horse's back. (We were driving Old Charley, well-known among all eastern Adventists). What had appeared to be a shallow creek we now saw was a deep and powerful stream. The swift current took the horse off his feet and floated both wagon and horse toward the mill-pond. Brother Cottrell on the foot-bridge, and I in the wagon lifted our hearts to God for help. I could not swim, and unless Providence intervened there was little hope for either the horse or me.

As we swept rapidly toward the mill-pond, the wagon wheels struck against a large rock and held the wagon fast until the horse regained his footing. He turned his head and cast a pitiful glance toward me. I shouted, "Charley, you must get me out of this!" As I pulled the rein to turn his head upstream, he gave two or three plunges with all his might toward the other side. He soon gained a good foothold and pulled the load safely to shore amid the cheering of a crowd that had gathered on the bank. We did not go far before we retired to a grove to thank God for deliverance from a watery grave.

Our second effort was in the city of Oswego, and Elder and Mrs. White were with me at this meeting. We were short of help erecting the tent. I overworked and became sick. It looked as though all the preaching would fall upon the Whites. Prayers were offered for me in the home of John Place, and I was immediately healed.

When in 1852, I accepted the message, we did not have the light on healthful living as now so clearly developed among this people. The testimonies spoke decidedly against the use of tea, coffee, and tobacco. But when there was sickness among us, we had not the light on the treatment of disease with natural remedies. We were requested to bring our sick ones to the Lord in prayer, following the rule in James 5. In the Rochester Church for many months, every case thus presented to the Lord was healed. This led some to conclude that every case thus presented to the Lord would be healed, but for this conclusion we had no support from either the Bible or Sister White.

About this time Nathaniel White (brother of James) was afflicted with tuberculosis, and prayers were offered for him. Although greatly blessed, he was wasting away. When the news reached our people, "Nathaniel White is dead," Sister Seely, who had taken part in several prayer seasons exclaimed, "He is not dead; he can't be for we have prayed for him!"

But to the Rochester company Sister White said, "The Lord has heard and answered our prayer in Nathaniel's case. He was gently let down to the grave in a manner that he is a burden to no one. God knew the future best, and the dangers to that ambitious young man. While in a prepared state, he has let him fall asleep."

At the time of Elder White's visit to Wisconsin in the spring of 1854, he became acquainted with Elders Stephenson and Hall who had been efficient First-day Adventist ministers. He encouraged them to come East and become more familiar with the work. So they attended a general meeting of our people at Rochester. While there they were anxious to learn the standing of the *Review*, and the whole situation was told them.

Through the *Review*, Elder White invited the Eastern brethren to raise means to purchase a tent for the feeble cause in Wisconsin so that Stephenson and Hall could more effectively reach the people. The tent was purchased and they returned with it, professing to be in full harmony with the cause. But by midsummer we learned that in their meetings they were seeking to prejudice the people against the *Review* and Elder and Mrs. White. Stephenson was using the information he had obtained from Elder White to prove that White was trying to build himself up, when those who knew him best knew his self-sacrificing labors were for the sole object of extending the cause of truth. While he was the legal owner of the *Review*, he never claimed it as his own. As soon as a legal publishing association was formed, he freely turned the whole thing over to the Seventh-day Adventists.

When Stephenson and Hall were First-day Adventists, they had accepted the theory of an "Age to Come," in which probation for sinners would continue beyond Christ's return. Their object was to have the *Review* publish their theories or they would destroy its influence. Very soon they began to write for the *Messenger*[1] and thus they lost their hold upon our people.

At the time of my healing at the home of Brother Place, Sister White was taken off in vision and was given important instruction for us regarding the Messenger of Truth. Five of us, White, Waggoner, Cornell, Frisbie and myself, had decided upon a line of attack against the slanderous assertions

---

1   Two disaffected Adventists, H. S. Case and C. P. Russell of Jackson, Michigan, published a paper called Messenger of Truth. The title "Age to Come" was associated with them after Stephenson and Hall joined them and promoted theories of an earthly millennial reign of Christ during which probation for sinners would continue.

in the Messenger. We had decided among ourselves without counsel with Sister White. After she came out of vision she said to her husband, "You brethren have made a mistake in your plans to refute the Messenger paper. When you answer one of their lies, they will make two more to match them. It is the trick of the enemy to keep you following them up and thus keep you from working with all the new interests that have arisen. Let the Messenger people alone, and pay no attention to their work, for in less than six weeks they will be at war among themselves. That paper will go down, and when they cease its publication, you will find that our ranks have doubled."

"All right," we agreed, "We will abandon our scheme and say no more about them in the *Review*." Up to that time the *Review* had rebutted their false statements. When the next *Review* appeared with nothing in it about the Messenger, they exulted, "Now the battle is fought. They dare not say anything against us." Then when the succeeding issues of the *Review* made no mention of their work, they boasted still stronger. But soon afterwards, two of their number who had been their best financial support withdrew. Their paper struggle on until 1857, then died for lack of support. When the paper went down, there were more than twice as many adherents to our cause as in 1855 when Sister White so predicted.

Leaving Oswego (with Bro. Cottrell as tent-master) we went to Ulysses, Pennsylvania, where W. S. Ingraham joined me in tent labor. Altogether our tent for that season was erected in nine places. At the Olcott meeting which was attended by Elder and Mrs. White, she gave us a testimony on the importance of continuing longer in one place. "It would be better and accomplish more good if there were fewer tent-meetings and a stronger force or company, with different gifts of labor. Then there should be a longer stay in a place where an interest is awakened. There has been too much haste in taking down the tent. Some begin to be favorably impressed, and there is need that persevering efforts be put forth till their minds become settled, and they commit themselves to the truth."

At a conference held in Battle Creek on the 28th and 29th of April, 1855, the brethren voted to invite Elder White to move the *Review* Office from Rochester to Battle Creek. Dan Palmer, Cyrenius Smith, J. P.

Kellogg, and Henry Lyon agreed to furnish $300 each to purchase a lot and erect a publishing office. They secured the lot on the south-east corner of West Main and Washington Streets, and erected a two-story wooden building 20 x 30 feet. The first number of the *Review* published here was *December* 4, 1855.

In May 1856, Brethren Ingraham, Cottrell and I started out again with the New York tent. After three weeks at Syracuse we moved to Rosevelt. At that meeting, having made up my mind that R. F. Cottrell ought to be preaching, I told him one Sunday that he must fill the one o'clock appointment, as I was going to get some rest. He consented supposing he would be alone in the effort.

After he was well started, I went to the tent back of the rostrum and sat down beside the wall to listen. When he concluded his sermon, he began to give out my appointment for five o'clock. I lifted the wall over my head and was inside the tent just as he said, "Brother Loughborough will speak at five o'clock." Then he saw me and added, "Here he is. Let him give out his own appointment."

Afterwards he asked, "Did you sit there all the time I was preaching?"

"No," I answered. "not inside the tent, but just outside, and now you've got to take a turn with us." From that time on he began preaching as well as writing the truth.

At that time there was no system established among Seventh-day Adventists for sustaining the ministry. If anyone cared to give them money, it was thankfully received, and the lack supplied by their hand labor. Due to these circumstances I was invited by Elder J. N. Andrews to go to Waukon, Iowa, where he could secure a small piece of land on which to grow supplies for his family, and could speak to the people in that new country as the way might open. So on October 4, 1856, J. T. Orton and I, with our families, left Rochester for Iowa in two lumber wagons.

From Buffalo we took the steamer to Detroit, then by freight train to Chicago. On the 11th, we started overland for Waukon, arriving November 20. I moved to Waukon without any intent of leaving the truth or the ministry.

We found things much different from what we expected. The country was so new and the inhabitants so scattered there was little chance of holding meetings. High prices soon began to diminish what little money I had. A cold winter was coming on, so I began laboring at carpenter work thinking to earn money to support my family, then start out and labor for the cause. I felt sad when I thought of the suffering cause of God. But worldly prospects brightened up before me. My heart began to reach out for treasures here, and I began to lose interest in the *Review*, and to lose love for the brethren. At times when about my work, solemn convictions would come to me that I must throw all my energies into the cause of God or die. As I struggled against these convictions, they became less and less.

We learned in the *Review* of early December, 1856, that Elder and Mrs. White had gotten as far west as Round Grove, Illinois and they were having very interesting meetings with Sabbathkeepers who had moved there from Vermont and other states. But we had little thought of their making a venture in the severe cold and deep snows of December to come with their sleigh nearly 200 miles to see us. In a vision given Sister White at Round Grove, December 9, they were instructed that they must go to Waukon, dig us out and get us into the field again.

Chapter 8

"What Doest Thou Here, Elijah?"

One day about Christmas time as Brother Mead and I were working on a store building in Waukon, a man looked up at me and inquired, "Do you know a carpenter around here by the name of Hosea Mead?"

"Yes, sir," I replied. "He's up here working with me."

Brother Mead said, "That's Elon Evert's voice!" Then he came and looked down. "Come down!" Everts shouted. "Brother and Sister White and Brother Hart are here in the sleigh!"

If these persons had dropped upon us from the skies, they would hardly have astonished us more. The ground was covered with three feet of snow plus several crusts which were not strong enough to bear up a horse. For more than a week all roads for 40 miles south of Waukon had been abandoned as impassable. The people had been waiting for the weather to moderate before attempting to open the roads. It looked as though one sleigh load, breaking their way through 40 miles of such snow, undertook a Herculean task.

As I reached the sleigh, Sister White greeted me with the question, "What doest thou here, Elijah?"

Shocked at such a question I replied, "I'm working with Brother Mead at carpenter work." Again she asked, "What doest thou here, Elijah?"

Now I was so embarrassed at her connecting my case with Elijah I did not know what to say. It was evident there was something back of this I should hear about.

Then she repeated the question a third time, "What doest thou here, Elijah?"

I was brought by these bare questions to very seriously consider Elijah hid in a cave away from the work of the Lord. Later on during the meetings here, I learned that she was instructed in a vision at Round Grove to greet me in this very manner. I assure you that the salutation thoroughly convinced me there would come a change and "go back" from the labor in which I was then engaged.

Meetings began in the home of Elder Andrews *December* 26, and continued until January 1, 1857. The Whites presented to us in a faithful manner the Laodicean message of Revelation 3:14–22. As the church began to receive the testimony, and to make confession of coldness and backslidings, light came in. We were encouraged to this heart-work by entreaties to return to the Lord and He would heal all our backslidings.

During the Waukon meetings, Sister White had three visions. Two were given the same evening under peculiar circumstances. There was a sister present who was in much sadness and almost on the brink of despair, feeling so keenly over the wrongs of her past life. In the first vision of the evening, Mrs. White was impressed to tell this sister that if she would take her stand, confessing her past wrongs to God, she would obtain forgiveness and, if faithful, need not look back of that night again. The sister did as she was bidden and light and glory came in.

Immediately sister White was again in vision and saw that the Lord had accepted the sister's confession, and that the past was forgiven. The sister then arose and gave glory to God.

Our facilities for entertaining company at that time were somewhat meager. It was 13 miles to a grist-mill. The winter's snow had closed in upon us suddenly, much sooner than expected. There was no flour in the neighborhood when our friends came. We were just about consuming our last loaves of genuine "bran bread." So for two days, all we had to offer them was meat, potatoes, and hulled corn. When the weather moderated, all the neighborhood turned out and broke the road to the mill, after which we had something a little better to serve our friends.

On the first day of January, 1867, I laid up my carpenter tools for good, said goodbye to our people in Waukon, and started with the Whites for Illinois. When we reached the Mississippi, the ice was again thoroughly frozen so that we passed over safely. When we arrived at

Galena, Illinois, Elder and Mrs. White took the train for Battle Creek while I went on with the brethren to Round Grove, and soon began a series of meetings in the Hickory Grove schoolhouse, three miles from the home of Josiah Hart. As a result of these meetings, a number of persons took their stand, among them the Andrews family, and some of the Colcord family. Robert Andrews and G. W. Colcord afterwards became ministers in the message.

That the ministerial work was not a source of great financial gain will be apparent to all when I state that for the first three months of labor in Illinois, I received my board and lodging, a buffalo robe overcoat, and ten dollars in money to pay my share of home expenses in Waukon where my wife was staying. On my return trip, I walked 26 miles with a heavy satchel on my back so as to have a little money left on reaching home.

In early June, I joined Brethren Hart and Everts with the Wisconsin tent at Mackford. A number of our people were living there who had come from Oswego, New York, and were anxious for their neighbors to hear the evidences of their faith. Many of the neighbors did accept the truth, and among them Rufus Baker. P. S. Thurston had been one of our ministers in Canada, but his wife was a member of another denomination. After two days of listening and careful study, she took a firm stand with her husband.

Philander Cady of Poy Sippi was then constructing a barn in the vicinity. He listened for a whole Sunday to the messages of the law and the Sabbath. Rejoicing in the light, he did not wish to keep it to himself. Near him lived John Matteson, a Scandinavian minister. They entered into an earnest study of the matter together, which resulted in Matteson's accepting, and at once presenting it to the people of his nationality.

From Mackford we went to Dodgeville for a three-week effort. Though a strong infidel town, somehow these infidels took a great interest in our meetings. One of them stated that this was the first religious meeting he had attended in 14 years. In those days we took no collections, but unknown to us, the infidels raised $50 for our expenses.

On leaving Dodgeville, we went with our tent to Green Vale, Illinois Here we met Moses Hull of Plum River. He had been a First-day Adventist minister and had accepted the message through reading. Wishing to know his ability as a public speaker, I invited him to speak on "The Christian's

Hope." This he did with acceptance by our people, and for some time he joined us in our labors.

After the harvest we put two tents into the field, one with Brother Ingraham, Hutchins, and Philips, while Brother Sperry and I took the other to White Rock. One very interested brother paid our bills for board and room at the tavern.

However, some young antagonists seemed intent on causing us trouble, but every move they made to create disturbance only enlisted the people in our favor. After the second evening these ruffians, talking loudly about the law of Moses, went out and got a lamb and, after cutting off his ear, threw him into the tent intending him (we suppose) as a sacrifice. During the last of our meetings we were in a schoolhouse close to the tent. These rude fellows pulled up over half of the small stakes, then attached large guys to the axle of a lumber wagon, thinking that the starting of the wagon would pull the tent over. But they were discovered in time.

Our efforts were continued until the fall rains and cool weather. I then returned to Waukon, and was glad to learn that George I. Butler, formerly a skeptic, had been soundly converted and had joined with the Sabbathkeepers in Waukon.

Soon after reaching home, I sold my horse and wagon and most of my household goods and moved to Battle Creek, reaching there the first of November. Our people had just completed their second meeting-house, 42 x 28 in size. The first one, 24 x 18 had been too small to accommodate the growing work. At a general gathering of our people on November 6, the house of worship was dedicated, and I was asked to give the first sermon. In west Battle Creek, Elder White obtained a cottage for me for $400.

After settling in Battle Creek in 1857, a little daughter was added to the family. The winter of 1857 was hard economically. Wheat was only sixty-five cents a bushel, and oats thirty-five. For the whole six months of that winter I received three ten-pound cakes of maple sugar, ten bushels of wheat, five bushels of apples, one-half of a small hog, one peck of beans, and four dollars in cash. Light had not come on health reform, nor was any system yet established for the support of the ministry.

In March 1858, Sister White said to her husband, "The Lord has shown me that if you call the ministers together and have J. N. Andrews come from

Waukon and hold a Bible class, you will find in the Scriptures a complete plan for supporting the ministry." Some may ask, "Why did not the Lord show her at once what the plan was?" My reply is, "Because He wanted our people to search it out in the Scriptures for themselves." During April of that year the Bible class was held in Battle Creek, after which our brethren said, "The tithing system is just as binding as it ever was." In introducing it, however, they called it "systematic benevolence on the tithing principle."

I spent the summer of 1858 in tent meetings in the state of Ohio—Green Springs, Gilboa, Lovett's Grove, Republic. Continuing the eastern journey with Elder and Mrs. White, we went to Rochester and Buck's Bridge, New York Our three-day meeting was very profitable for that company. There is a story in connection with that meeting which illustrates the zeal of some of our people. One sister came to Mrs. White much burdened and said, "I like Elder Loughborough's preaching, but I am sorry to see him following the fashions of the day."

"In what respect?" Mrs. White inquired.

"Why," said the woman, "in the manner of shaving his beard. He leaves a mustache upon his upper lip, and a goatee upon his chin."

Mrs. White replied, "If that is all your trouble about him, I can relieve your mind at once. He does not shave at all. He lets all the beard grow that God has given him, and I suppose when the Lord gives him any more, he will let that grow, too."

While on the Eastern trip with Elder and Mrs. White, she said to me one day, "There is a wonderful vision that was once presented to me, but it does not come distinctly before me so I can relate it. It is just wonderful!"

After our return to Michigan in October, there was a general three-day meeting of our people in the church on Van Buren Street. The climax came on Sunday, the last day of the meeting. It was expected that J. N. Andrews would speak at 10:30 a.m. and J. H. Waggoner at 2 p.m.

In a social meeting at 9 a.m., Sister White arose to speak. Her countenance was lighted up with power of God, and she began to tell us things we had never heard from her lips before. It was the vision of the great controversy, beginning with Satan's revolt in heaven. As it opened then and there before her, she related it to us. As she spoke, the mighty power of God filled all the room where we were sitting. Some expressed afterwards the sensation we felt, "It seemed as though heaven and earth were running together."

Those present could never forget the evident presence of the power of God accompanying her relating of the great controversy with the final triumph of right, and the defeat of Satan.

As the subject opened up before her, Sister White talked until noon. No hint was made that anyone else had an appointment. It was evident to all that it was the Lord's meeting, and almost spellbound we listened to the instruction the Lord had for us. While she was earnestly relating the facts, a Presbyterian deacon, a next-door neighbor of mine, was passing the church on his way to his own meeting in the city. He had never been known to attend our meetings, but attracted by the sound of Sister White's voice, he stepped inside and sat down. There he sat, listening with almost breathless attention the whole forenoon.

When Sister White was at last told, "It is noon," she responded, "Well, I have only gotten started in relating what opens before me." Elder White inquired, "Will you go on with your talk at one o'clock?" She replied that she would. Promptly at one o'clock all were present to hear the remainder of the vision; and among the rest, the deacon sat in a seat near the front of the congregation. The afternoon talk continued for four hours. Our people remarked that never before in their lives had they known such a day. This was the first time that Sister White related her vision of the great controversy between Christ and Satan.

Chapter 9

Organization and the Civil War

The year 1860 marked a new and important feature in the advancement of the work. The printing outfit of hand press and type, valued at $700, which was paid for by donations of our people and moved to Battle Creek in 1855, was augmented in 1857 by the addition of a power press. In 1860, the publishing plant of the *Review and Herald*, aside from the building, was worth $5,000. While Elder White was legally owner of this property, he did not call it his own but said, "This is the property of the church. I am only managing it."

Satan moved upon some enemies to say, "You see how Elder White is building up a property of his own from the liberalities of the people." To defeat such insinuations and provide proper management of a rapidly growing cause, the elder was impressed that some plan should be devised for conducting the business of the church. To introduce the matter to our people he published an article in the *Review* of February 28, 1860.

Responding to White's request, I wrote an article for the March 8 *Review* in which I said, "What I understand is necessary to remedy all the defects in this matter is to organize in such a manner that we can hold the property legally…. If it is not wrong to hold farms and village lots in a lawful manner, neither is it wrong to hold church property in the same way."

But strangely an article appeared in the March 22 *Review* by an esteemed brother claiming that Elders White and Loughborough wished to make a name like the builders of the tower of Babel. He claimed we were going into Babylon, uniting church and state. In the next two issues of the paper, Elder White gave a full reply, showing that while it is not right to resort to the civil arm to enforce the worship of God, "the Lord's goods can be managed in this state of things only according to the laws of the country," and it was "vain talk of church property" if the church did not hold it legally.

During the summer of 1860, this question was freely discussed in the *Review*. In a general meeting of our people held in Battle Creek from September 28 to October 1, there was a candid consideration of the subject, and a full, free discussion of legal organization. It was voted to organize legally a publishing association as soon as possible. The conference also discussed the subject of a name for our people. This again brought diversity of opinion. When "Church of God" was proposed, it was objected to because it gave none of the distinctive features of our faith, while the name "Seventh-day Adventist" would not only set forth our faith in the near coming of Christ, but would also show we observed the Seventh-day Sabbath. So unanimous was the assembly in favor of the latter name, only one man voted against it.

At a council held in Battle Creek on June 9, one important topic was the distribution of labor. Elder M. E. Cornell was assigned to Ohio for the summer, and I was to join Elder T. M. Steward with the Wisconsin tent. Our first meeting was at Marquette, Wis., on the shore of a beautiful lake, having Rufus Baker as tent master. Our meetings continued here from June 29 to August 4, Nearly a score accepted the truth, among them the Hallecks, earnest missionary workers.

Just at that time an unfortunate era entered our cause in Wisconsin. From New England came a professed Seventh-day Adventist minister, Solomon Wellcome, with a fanciful theory on the subject of sanctification. I could not accept his teaching, but Steward was anxious for Wellcome to speak. So on the evening after the Sabbath, July 14, he took the service. It seemed to me that his thrusts against obedience to the law, and his exaltation of sanctification when "all our thoughts would be from the Lord," would lead to fanaticism. Unfortunately, the new doctrine took root there and led to what Sister White labeled "the most unreasonable, foolish, wild fanaticism that ever cursed Wisconsin."

At another council in Battle Creek, September 28 to October 1, it was arranged that I should return to Wisconsin, and Elder White hold meetings in New York and Ohio. Accordingly, we each began to lay plans, but on the evening of October 6, Elder White with Elder Cornell came to my home on Champion St. and said, "I feel strangely about our proposed trips. I don't feel free about going East, and don't know what it means."

After an earnest prayer season we rose from our knees with our minds entirely changed, he with the conviction to go West, and I that I should go East. We changed our appointments without any knowledge of the condition of things in the West. When Elder White reached Mauston, Wisconsin, he found a terrible fanaticism developing. I had no experience in meeting fanaticism, but Elder White's experience enabled him to labor effectively with those people.[1]

While on this tour, the Lord gave Elder White an impressive dream. As he prayed for the cause in Battle Creek, there seemed to come before him his little child, about six-weeks old, in great distress with a badly swollen head. The night following, he dreamed of trouble with three banks in Battle Creek in which the *Review* office had deposited funds for the erection of an additional building. He dreamed he saw a banker who was considered the soundest financially, selling second-hand shoes in an old, dilapidated building over the mill race.

He wrote his wife that he feared all was not well with the babe. I handed the letter to Mrs. White, and as she read it she looked down at the plump, laughing child and said, "I don't think he would call that child very sick if he should see it now." That night the child was taken with erysipelas, and in a day or two both eyes were swollen shut. At the request of Mrs. White, I telegraphed Lovias Hall, Morrison, Illinois, "Tell Elder White to come home immediately. Child dangerously sick."

When Elder White arrived at the home of Eli Wick at Clyde, Illinois, he asked if there was a telegram for him. He said, "I don't expect to fill my appointment here. I look for a telegram from home announcing that my child is very sick." Ten minutes later, Lovias Hall drove up in his sulky with the dispatch, and White immediately left for home.

---

1   Elder and Mrs. Steward of Mauston had accepted Solomon Wellcome's theory of instantaneous sanctification, and were presenting it from church to church. Mrs. Steward claimed the gift of prophecy and related visions countering those of Mrs. White

When I met him at the train, his first question was about the child. Then he related the dream about the banks and asked if I had any fears of their being unsafe. On being assured that I had not, he said he was going to get stone, brick, lumber, etc. for the new building, and paper for the *Review*, so as to draw all the association money from the banks, for he was confident they were going down. The child died soon after Elder White's return, and every one of the banks failed.

On Sabbath, January 12, 1861, Elders Waggoner, Smith, White and his wife, and I attended the dedication of the Parkville, Michigan church. At the close of White's sermon, his wife gave a stirring exhortation. As she sat down in her chair, she was taken off in vision which lasted about twenty minutes. The church was crowded and indeed solemn.

Dr. Brown was present, a spiritualistic medium and physically strong. He declared that Mrs. White's visions were due to spirit mediumship, and that if she had one when he was present, he could bring her out of it in one minute.

Elder White invited all who wished to do so to come and examine her while in vision. Someone challenged, "Doctor, go ahead and do as you said you would." White then asked, "Is there a doctor here? We always like to have physicians examine Mrs. White in vision."

The doctor started quite bravely, but before he got halfway to Mrs. White, he turned deathly pale and shook like a leaf. He was urged to go on and make the examination. As soon as this was completed, he made his way rapidly to the door and seized the knob to go out. Those standing by prevented him saying, "Go back and do as you said you would do." Elder White, seeing the doctor trying to get out the door, said, "Will the doctor please report to the audience?" He replied, "Her heart and pulse are regular, but there is not a particle

of breath in her body." Then in great agitation he again grasped the door knob. The people nearby asked, "Doctor, what is it?" He replied, "God only knows! Let me out of here!"

After coming out of vision, Sister White arose and said, "There is not a single person here who ever dreamed of the trouble that is coming upon this land. People are making sport of the secession of South Carolina, but I have just been shown that a large number of states are going to join that state, and there will be a most terrible war. In this vision I have seen large armies of both sides gathered on the field of battle. I heard the booming of the cannon, and saw the dead and dying on every hand…." Then looking slowly around the church she continued, "There are those in this house who will lose sons in that war."

The vision was given just three months before the first gun was fired on Fort Sumter.

Near the stand sat Judge Osborne, whose wife was a Sabbath-keeper. By his side sat Mr. Shelhouse, owner of a large woolen factory, both leading men in the Republican party. When Mrs. White told what was coming, they looked at me and shook their heads. One year from that time when I spoke in the same church, these two men sat together again. My subject was spiritual gifts. In illustration of the gift as manifest by Sister White, I referred to the vision of January 12, 1861. This time, these men did not shake their heads, but instead their faces were in their handkerchiefs, and they sobbing bitter tears. Alas! One had lost his only son in the war. The other had lost a son on the battlefield, and another son was in a Southern prison. The elder of the Parkville Church later told me that he knew of six or seven others there who had lost sons in the war.

During the summer of 1861, Isaac Sanborn and I held tent meetings in northern Illinois and southern Wisconsin. Our first meetings were at Clinton Junction, June 8 to July 7. Under the circumstances of the national struggle, we felt it advisable to have on the tent pole a flag of the stars and stripes. While there, soldiers who were gathering to their regiments would come to this place and have to wait several hours for a train on another road. Instead of leaving them to camp in the hot sun, we invited them to enjoy the seats and shade of our tent. Before they would leave, they would ask us to speak to them. We tried to give them some wholesome advice, and had prayer with them for which they gave most hearty thanks.

Our third meeting was held at Davistown, Wisconsin, beside the village commons. A company of soldiers was drilling on the grounds while we erected the tent. It was our custom to put up our flag as soon as the canvas and tent wall were in place. When we erected our pole with the flag rope attached, Brother Decker, our tent master, overheard the captain ask, "Boys, what kind of flag is going up there? We must watch and see." When we learned this we said, "Brother Decker, run up the flag at once!"

Captain Cain stopped his drill, came to us and said, "Gentlemen, your property will be protected, for Lincoln has given orders that the soldiers protect all property over which the United States flag floats." True to their promise, when our meetings opened, two men on sentry duty marched back and forth, giving each other the hand salute.

We learned that a war rally was appointed on the commons for Sabbath, August 24. The owner who had given us free use of the ground upon which the tent was pitched, and the man who owned the seats asked us for the use of the tent for a war meeting, so the people would not have to stand in the hot sun. There flashed into my mind the thought, "What if our church at Avon, only a few miles away, learns that a war rally was held in our tent the very first Sabbath of our series? We will risk an explanation to them rather than the wrath of the people for refusing them shade on their own land." We did not stop to parley over the matter, for had we said "No" we might as well pack up and leave. So we replied, "Occupy the tent, and welcome."

Although we knew their war meetings were opened with prayer, it did not occur to us that they might ask us to take part, but at their first meeting I was asked to offer prayer. I know God helped me to pray with a tender heart, not only for the preservation of those liberties for which our fathers fought, but for the soldiers who were risking their lives in the war.

In September 1862, the Michigan Conference held its first session in Monterey. Here for the first time was presented the idea of churches being received into conferences, as members were voted into churches. At this conference also a plan was adopted of paying ministers a weekly sum for their services. The Michigan Conference for the year just then closed, settled with salaries varying from $4 to $7 per week.

In October of this year, Moses Hull, who was considered a good debater, held a discussion in Paw Paw, Michigan with a noted Spiritualist named Jamieson. At that time Hull partially fell under the influence of satanic delusion. On November 5, several persons assembled at my home to talk with him. At the close of the interview, we had a prayer season, and while in a kneeling posture, Mrs. White was taken off in vision. Some of the things she saw at this time are recorded in *Testimonies*, volume 1, page 426.

My next-door neighbor, Mr. Diagneau, had never before seen her in vision, and so used many tests to satisfy himself that she did not breathe, that she knew nothing of what transpired around her, and that she was controlled by a superior power.

Mr. Diagneau was a strong man, a stone mason. While in vision Mrs. White would clasp her hands together upon her chest, and he could not by the utmost exertion raise one finger sufficiently to get his thumb and finger between her finger and hand. Almost the next moment she would unclasp her hands and gracefully move her arm and hand toward the subject she seemed to be viewing.

While her arm was extended, Elder White said, "Brother Diagneau, that looks like an easy motion, and as though you, a strong man, could easily bend her arm. You can try it if you wish." He then placed his knee in the bend of her elbow, and taking hold of the extended hand with both his hands, pulled backward with all his might without bending it in the least. He commented, "I would as soon try to bend an iron bar as that arm." Before he had closed the sentence, her arm passed gracefully back

to her chest, but with a force that slid his feet on the floor while trying to resist. He at once admitted that there was superhuman strength connected with the vision, for he well knew Mrs. White to be a woman of delicate health.

On November 24 1862, two meetings were held at the same hour in the home of William Wilson of Greenville, for the purpose of organizing two churches. The meeting for the Greenville Church was conducted by Elder and Mrs. White, while Elder Byington and I met in another room with the West Plains Church. While we were busy with preliminary work, we could hear Mrs. White's voice in the other room. We were having some difficulties when, just at the opportune time, Mrs. White opened the door and said, "Brother Loughborough, I see by looking over this company that I have testimonies for some of the persons present. When you are ready, I will come in and speak." Since this was just the time we needed help, she came in. Aside from Elder Byington and me, she knew the names of only three persons in the room. The others were strangers except as they had been presented to her in vision.

As she arose to speak, she said, "You will have to excuse me in relating what I have to say if I describe your persons, as I do not know your names. As I see your faces, there comes before me what the Lord has shown me concerning you. That man in the corner with one eye (someone spoke, "His name is Pratt.") makes high professions, and great pretensions of religion, but he has never been converted. Do not take him into the church in his present condition for he is not a Christian. He spends much of his time idling about the shops and stores arguing the theory of the truth, while his wife at home has to cut the firewood, look after the garden, etc. He makes promises in his bargains that he does not fulfill. His neighbors have no confidence in him. It would be better for the cause of religion for him to say nothing about it."

She continued, "This aged brother (as she pointed to him some one said, "Brother Barr") was shown to me in direct contrast with the other man. He is very exemplary in his life, careful to keep his promises, and provides well for his family. He hardly ventures to speak of the truth to his neighbors for fear he will mar the work and do harm. He does not know how the Lord can be so merciful as to forgive his sins, and thinks himself unfit to belong to the church." She then said, "Brother Barr, the Lord bade me tell you that you have confessed all the sins you know of, and that He forgave your sins long ago, if you will only believe it."

Brother Barr looked up with a smile, "Has He?"

"Yes," responded Mrs. White, "and I was told to say to you, Come along and unite with the church and, as you have opportunity, speak a word in favor of the truth. It will have good effect for your neighbors have confidence in you."

He replied, "I will."

Continuing, she said, "If Mr. Pratt could for a time take a position similar to that of Brother Barr, it would do him good."

The moment the meeting closed, Mr. Pratt stated with vehemence, "I tell you, there is no use trying to go with this people and act the hypocrite. You can't do it!"

In the November 5 vision, statements were also made concerning Moses Hull. "Brother Hull has been dealt with faithfully. He has felt that he was too much restrained, that he could not act out his own nature. While the power of truth in all its force influenced him, he was comparatively safe, but break the force and power of truth upon his mind, and there is no restraint, the natural propensities take the lead, and there is no stopping place…. He was represented to me as standing upon the brink of an awful gulf, ready to leap. If he takes the leap, it will be fatal; his eternal destiny will be fixed."

The following winter Mr. Hull preached some in Michigan, seeking by this means to banish his doubts. In the spring of 1863, he accompanied me in tent meetings in New England, but during the whole time he had seasons of doubting and rallying. On September 20, he gave a sermon on the trials, conflicts, and victories of those who battle against sin. At the close of his remarks he told the congregation not to look to him, as his course would not affect the truth. After the meeting he said to me, "Tomorrow I shall leave for Ligonier, Indiana, where my people are. I shall not preach anymore." And so he did. When I next heard from him, he was advocating Spiritualism.

Chapter 10

The Marion Rebellion

In May 1865, the General Conference council on the distribution of labor decided that I go with Elder and Mrs. White in some meetings in Wisconsin, Illinois, and Iowa, and then labor among the churches in Iowa. At the time of our conference in Battle Creek we were rejoicing in the fact that the four years of terrible civil were over, and that now the coast was clear for a rapid advancement of the third angel's message. Little did we think that right in our midst, at the time of the conference, there were those on the ground who were gathering material with which to start another rebellion in the ranks of Seventh-day Adventists.

At this conference were two or three brethren accompanied by their wives who were not in the truth. They were dressed in worldly fashion and wore jewelry. Here were also Elders Snook and Brinkerhoff from Iowa, who had already (secretly) been sowing seeds of discord in their conference. Then, without taking pains to learn who the ladies in worldly dress were, they returned with great stories of the pride of the Battle Creek Church, and how they saw them decorated with feathers and jewelry. They also trumped up objections to the testimonies, and set out to cause division in our ranks in Iowa.

Of all this we knew nothing until we reached Monroe, Wisconsin (June 9). There Elder Ingraham showed Elder White a letter he received from Snook which said, "Brother Ingraham, what do you think of striking out on the old plan of the independence of the churches?…" In this Elder White at once spotted rebellion, and throwing off conference organization. When we reached Pilot Grove, where a spring session of the Iowa Conference was to be held, we learned that Snook and Brinkerhoff were teaching that the message would go forward as soon as it was rid of Sister White's testimonies.

When we met in conference with our people at Pilot Grove, Elder White proposed that, before entering upon any business, there be an investigation of the charges made by Snook and Brinkerhoff. They elected me chairman of that meeting, and we devoted a full day (June 30) to the problem. The two men stated their objections, and either

Elder or Mrs. White made reply. At 5 p.m. both men admitted that their objections were fully answered and that they had no more. A day or so later I saw each of them, separately, hand to Elder White written confessions of their wrong course, then on Sunday, before a large audience of outside parties, Snook said that he had been serving the devil in his opposition to the Whites.

But after a few days, B. F. Snook's objections revived. He began to communicate with Brinkerhoff, and that ended his labors in our ranks, and they were again on their scheme of "independence of the churches." However, this did not assume its final fighting for several months. Meanwhile I labored with the Iowa churches. With reluctance I parted from Elder White, but duty called to different fields, and so our journeyings together, which had been of great encouragement to me, came to a close.

July 17, I left Marion for Waukon, and in passing over the railroad in Dubuque, I witnessed some of the ravages of the Wapsipinicon River which had risen 12 to 15 feet during the continuous rains. Large fields of corn and splendid gardens in the valleys had been swept away. Nearly every railroad bridge west of Dubuque was carried away. And when the water fell to its usual depth, old and safe fords had been gullied out to the extent that quite a number of teams and persons were drowned in the new gulfs.

On Friday, July 28, Elder George Butler took Elder Brinkerhoff and me in his carriage to West Union. When we came to Cleremont, we found the bridge over Turkey River gone and the fords impassable. The only means of crossing was in small row boats. It was only two hours from the time of our next meeting, and it was seven miles from the opposite side of the stream.

Since it was 20 miles to the nearest bridge, we decided to cross in the skiff. Our baggage, the harness, and wagon seats were first taken across.

Then the wagon was drawn astride a skiff with the wheels in the water. One man got into the boat to keep the wagon balanced. Another skiff with two men in it was rowed out, one man holding onto the tongue of our wagon and the other rowing with all his might up the stream. Next, they swam the horses over one at a time. Last, with some trembling, we entered the skiff, and were soon on the other shore.

On August 8, I traveled by stage 35 miles over very bad roads to Blairstown, where I found I must remain till morning before I could take the train. Here I had no place to stay but a small country tavern nearly filled with drunken hog-drivers. They caroused all night, and had three regular fist fights before midnight. I got no rest to speak of that night. The next morning I took the train 75 miles to Nevada. Here I found no food fit for a human being to eat, but did the best I could then started for Fort Des Moines by stage, 35 miles. The roads were in such a terrible state that it took five hours to cover the first ten miles of the journey.

At the time of our labors in Iowa, both Elder White and I were laboring beyond our better judgment. On the morning of August 24, I stepped off the train at Eddyville, expecting to go with Brother Kaufman a few miles out to preach a funeral sermon for a sister who had been buried a few days before. The brother handed me a telegram which read: "Elder White paralyzed. Come to Battle Creek immediately." The conductor held the train for me to secure my ticket, and I went on to Battle Creek. When I arrived there and laid off my active labor, my brain was so congested that I could not bear the jar of walking, except on tiptoes.

In Battle Creek I met Dr. Lay, a devoted church member who had visited Jackson's "water cure" in Dansville, New York, that he might learn their methods. After Elder White's stroke, he thought it best for the elder to go to Dansville for treatment, and on looking over my case decided that I, too, needed water treatment and rest. So on September 14, the Whites and I, accompanied by Dr. Lay started for the "Home on the Hillside" at Danville, where we stayed until *December* 7. After six weeks I recovered from the brain congestion, but remained with the Whites, taking them and others out for rides with a borrowed team and carriage.

On *December* 7, we went to Rochester and were courteously entertained in the home of Bradley Lamson until January 1, 1866, when

Elder White and family returned to Battle Creek. For three weeks Elder Andrews, Elder and Mrs. Orton, and others met with us daily at Lamsons to pray for Elder White. On Christmas Day, the Rochester church observed a fast, with three meetings in the city during the day, then we met again in the evening at Lamson's to pray with Elder White. It was a powerful season. In the midst of it, Sister White had a vision, and Elder White was greatly blessed. In relating the vision Sister White said, "Satan's purpose was to destroy my husband, and bring him down to the grave. Through these earnest prayers, his power has been broken."

By the time of my return to Battle Creek in the spring of 1866, Snook and Brinkerhoff had drawn off 45 of the 60 members of the Marion Church. They also gave energy to the Messenger and Hope of Israel parties, and were zealously fighting the testimonies of Sister White. They started a paper called The Advent and Sabbath Advocate. But before many months had passed, both men dropped interest in the Advocate and gave up the Sabbath. Brother Starr of Iowa told me that the day he was baptized, Brinkerhoff was present, and met him as he came up out of the water. Shaking hands with him he said, "I am glad to see you take your stand with this people.

They have the truth and I am sorry I ever left them…. It's too late for me to rejoin them. I am a lost man."

The Advocate, however, was continued by a man named William Long. But how could he be leader of a flock without an organization? They chose the name "Church of God" and soon organized churches and conferences, and finally a general conference with headquarters at Stanberry, Missouri.

From January until April 3, 1866, I remained in western New York, then returned to my home in Michigan and found Elder White still quite feeble. As the time for the General Conference session was drawing near, and Elder White unable to carry the burden as in former years, it was decided to appoint four days of fasting and prayer (May 9–12) for Elder White and for heavenly wisdom in the coming sessions of The General Conference, the Publishing Association, and the Michigan Conference (May 16–21). These meetings were held in the church and in a fifty-foot tent. On the morning of May 19, Sister White read to us for the first time the following testimony: "Our people should have an institution of their own, under their own control, for the benefit of the diseased and suffering among us.... Such an institution, rightly conducted, would be the means of bringing our views before many whom it would be impossible for us to reach by the common course of advocating the truth."

When the testimony was read to our people, the question arose, "How can we, in our condition of limited means, obtain and control a health institution?" Elder White was in critical health, so the matter seemed to fall upon the Michigan conference committee of which I was president. After agreeing to proceed in faith, I drew up a subscription paper, and went first to J. P. Kellogg who, in bold print, pledged $500.

In a few days we had secured the residence of Judge Graves with nine acres of land for $6,000. This is where the Battle Creek Sanitarium now stands. A two-story building with two rooms above and two below for treatment rooms and water tank, was erected. On September 5, 1866, the institution was formally opened for patients, having Drs. Lay and Byington as physicians, two helpers and one patient; being less than four months from the time the subject was first mentioned to our people. In August we began the publication of a sixteen-page monthly journal, The Health Reformer.

When we began to receive payments for shares in the enterprise, it became necessary to form a legal organization, so I counseled with lawyers Dibble and Rhine. They told us there was no law for our case except the law for mining and manufacturing corporations, and such law provided for payment of dividends to stockholders. Thinking we must follow the law, we provided for a dividend of net earnings. When our first report was made in the spring of 1867, Sister White at once said, "This is not the course we are to take in managing our health institutions. The light given me is that the earnings of the institution should go to the building up of the institution, and for charity work for the needy afflicted." Having received this additional light, we moved to remedy matters, and requested all who could to donate their profits to the institution. To this they readily assented.

At the General Conference of 1866, it was decided that some member of the General Conference committee should attend the state conferences of the Central and Western states, and that Elders A. C. and D. T. Bourdeau should labor in the West, especially in Iowa. So on June 5, in company with the Bourdeau brothers, I left for the Iowa state conference at Pilot Grove. From there I went to Illinois and Wisconsin. Then I returned to Battle Creek, but on the way held meetings with the little company of 12 members in the great city of Chicago.

Since most medical works are large and expensive, it was decided that a small book should be prepared, compiled from the larger works, containing those things essential to aid the common reader in line with the testimony given us. The director of the Health Reform Institute requested me to prepare the manuscript with the understanding that he would carefully examine and criticize it.

In between state conferences and various board meetings, it took one year to complete it. It was entitled Home Handbook of Health and totaled 228 pages. An edition of 3,000 was printed, bound in cloth, and sold for $.75 a copy.

On June 24, 1867, after the birth of a daughter, my wife was taken with a congestive chill, and within an hour from the birth of the child she was dead. Thus suddenly was I separated from her to whom I had been happily united for sixteen and one-half years. So I was left with a three-year-old son, and a helpless babe. Brother and Sister Myron Cornell kindly cared for little Mary for one year, and my brother and his family came from New York, occupied my house and cared for my boy.

Obituary of Mary Loughborough from *Review* of July 2, 1867

Mary J. Walker was born in Troy, New York, June 17, 1832. She was bereft of her father when but a few days old. A widowed mother still survives. She experienced religion under the labors of Eld. E. R. Pinney, of Rochester, New York, in 1849, who also now rests in hope. She was married to Eld. J. N. Loughborough in 1851, by whom she had five children, two of them still living. With her husband she embraced the truth of the third message under the labors of Eld. J. N. Andrews, in Rochester, New York, September 1852. She traveled with her husband in most of the States where there are Sabbathkeepers, and is the "Sister L." referred to in *Spiritual Gifts*, volume 2, p. 220. She died at the age of 35 years and 7 days.

An injury received by a fall some two weeks since, was probably the immediate cause of her death. On the day of her decease she gave birth to twin daughters, one of them, as it is supposed from the cause above mentioned, being dead.

On the occasion of the funeral, the 26th inst. Bro. Hutchins spoke from 1 Thess. 4:14. So we left her in Oak Hill cemetery, a new treasure committed to the tomb, there to slumber with her little one sweetly pillowed on her arm, till the Lifegiver shall return to rescue his jewels from the dominion of the enemy.

Chapter 11

Pioneering at Petaluma

Before 1868, Seventh-day Adventists had confined their efforts to the northeastern portion of the United States. In the late fifties, a Mrs. Morehouse accepted the truth in Missouri, and with her family made the five-month trip by ox-team to settle near Pendleton, Oregon. She was the first Seventh-day Adventist west of the Rockies. To Battle Creek she sent frequent appeals for a laborer. Her requests were answered in the *Review*, "Be patient. Laborers may come sometime, but not yet."

In the spring of 1859, Merritt G. Kellogg, half-brother of Dr. J. H. Kellogg, left Michigan with a company of gold seekers. After a five-month trip, he landed in San Francisco, and received employment as a carpenter at good wages. About 1864, J. W. Cronkite, a shoemaker, left Michigan for San Francisco via the isthmus, thinking to support himself by his trade, and by circulation of tracts do some missionary work. These few souls had Sabbath meetings in the home of B. G. St. John, a Baptist friend on Minna St. Anxious to see the message proclaimed publicly, this company raised $133 in gold, and sent it to Battle Creek accompanied by an earnest request for a minister.

During the winter of 1867–68, the Lord gave me a number of dreams about laboring in California. I dreamed of taking a ship in New York and riding down to the Isthmus, then taking another ship to California and there holding tent meetings. In my dreams that winter I suppose I took that trip via the Isthmus at least twenty times. About the same time, the mind of D. T. Bourdeau was exercised in a similar manner. He was so certain he would be sent to a distant field that he sold all his household goods and came to Battle Creek with his wife to attend the General Conference in May.

Most of the meetings during the latter part of the conference were for the ministers. When it came to the distribution of labor, calls were made from Wisconsin, and several other states. Then finally, M. G. Kellogg made a very strong plea for someone to go to California. The people were amazed for California then seemed so far off, almost out of the world. Elder White requested the ministers to earnestly seek the Lord for guidance as to which field to occupy. When the report was called for on May 18, all the ministers responded except Elder Bourdeau and me. Elder White then asked, "Has anyone had any impressions of duty about California?" Then I arose and for the first time stated my impressions and dreams about California.

Elder White then remarked, "When the Lord sent forth His servants, He sent them two by two. Is there another whose mind has been led to that field?" Then Elder Bourdeau arose and stated his feelings, and that he had come to the meeting with his companion and all his remaining earthly possessions, ready to go where the conference might direct. Elder White then said, "Will Brethren Bourdeau and Loughborough pray over this together and separately until the day the *Review* goes to press, that they may be sure of the mind of the Lord in this matter." We most earnestly sought the Lord, and on the morning of May 31, Elder White asked, "Brethren, what is the decision?" Our united reply was, "California or nothing." He at once penned the statement for the *Review* calling for $1,000 to secure a tent and send us to California.

The railroad across the plains then lacked 500 miles of completion, so it was necessary to go by water via Central America. We left Battle Creek, June 8, spending two weeks in New York, purchasing a tent and supplies for the journey. Here also I was united in marriage to Margaret A. Newman, Elder Bourdeau performing the ceremony.

A friend in Battle Creek, who had been three times through the isthmus, advised me, "You will be wise to secure your ticket several days before you sail. There is competition between the American Line and the Pacific mail. Go to New York the day after the Mail Line ship has sailed, and get the American figures first. With these figures, go to the Mail Line and they will give you much lower rates." We followed his advice and were able to secure a good room in the center of the ship for $467.50 for the five of us, just $212.50 less than what we would have paid had our friend not advised us.

As we boarded the boat, Elder Bourdeau's $5 hat got knocked into the water, which he fretted about every day until we reached Panama. Leaving New York June 24, we arrived at Aspinwal, July 3, at 9:00 a.m. At eleven we were on our way to Panama by rail and arrived at 3 p.m. and were taken by tug boat to the steamer anchored one mile off shore. We were told the steamer would soon leave for California, but it lay at anchor for two days. This steamer, "The Golden Gate," was the largest the company owned. The next boat to make the trip was a small one, so our ship took on all the slow freight it could to make it easier for the next ship.

Our steamer arrived at San Francisco at 10;00 a.m. Sabbath, July 18, after 24 days travel from New York. As Brother Kellogg had given us the address of the St. Johns family, with the assurance they would entertain us, Elder Bourdeau went to prospect while I remained with the family until the trunks came from the steamer. He soon returned stating he had found the few Sabbath-keepers just assembling for meeting, and that they adjourned until we should arrive. An expressman took us with our trunks to St. John where we were made welcome, and had a brief Sabbath meeting as our introduction to California.

When Elder White made the call in the *Review* for $1,000 to send us to California with a new tent, one of the New York City journals immediately grasped it as a news item, and stated in their paper that two evangelists were about to sail for California to hold religious services in a large tent.

In Petaluma there was a group of worshippers who called themselves "Independents," who had separated from various churches, feeling they could not fellowship with their formality and pride. When they saw the notice of the evangelists coming with a tent, they prayed that if these were the Lord's servants, they might have a prosperous journey.

The night following their prayer meeting, one of their prominent members, Mr. Wolf, was given a very impressive dream. He saw gloom and darkness settled all over the surrounding country. While considering this, he saw two men building a fire which brought cheer to the inhabitants. As the fire blazed brightly and his people were rejoicing in the light, he saw all the ministers of Petaluma come with brush and grass, throwing it upon the fire to extinguish the flames. But the more they tried to put out the fire, the brighter it burned. While the ministers were trying to put out the first fire, the two men had started a second. This process was repeated until the men had kindled five fires. The ministers lamented, "The more we put out the fires, the brighter they burn. There is no use trying to publicly oppose these men for they get the advantage of us every time." Then Mr. Wolf dreamed that the two men were the ones who were coming with the tent. He related his dream to his brethren, telling them he must see these evangelists on their arrival for if they were the men of his dream, he would surely know them.

We were not expecting our tent until two weeks after our arrival. What was our surprise on the morning of July 20, as Elder Bourdeau and I took a walk to the Pacific Mail wharf, to see the sacks containing our tent had come on the same steamer with us! Here was another providence. Our tent was among the extra freight put on at Panama for which we had paid only slow freight rates.

Since our tent had come, we hurried to get side poles, ropes, lamps, and fixtures ready. We had the tent moved to St. Johns and began to study and pray about where to erect it. The few Sabbath-keepers were anxious that our first effort be held there, but when we prayed about it, our minds were impressed to go to the northwest, away from San Francisco. With all our searching in the city, we found only one place that could be secured, and the owner of the lot asked $40 a month. That settled the question about beginning in San Francisco at that time.

Thus matters stood until July 27, when Mr. Hough, one of the Independents of Petaluma, called at St. Johns and inquired if there were two ministers with a tent staying with him. How did he so quickly find us in a city then numbering 175,000? On his way down he had been impressed to go at once to the Pacific Mail and inquire if a tent had come on the last steamer from Panama. As he asked, "Where was the tent?" the very drayman who had moved the tent, came into the warehouse and directed him to Minna St. So in thirty minutes from the time Mr. Hough landed in San

Francisco on the Petaluma steamer, he had found us.

We went to Petaluma the next day. On our arrival, Mr. Hough met us and said, "You will stay at my house tonight, but it is arranged for you to take dinner at Mr. Wolf's." We learned afterwards that this was planned so that Mr. Wolf could see if the two men were the ones he had seen in his dream. When he saw us coming, he said to his wife, "There they are! Those are the identical men I saw in the dream." That settled the matter for that company, and they did all they could in securing rooms for us, and arranging for our tent meetings.

On August 3, we settled in housekeeping rooms belonging to one of the Independents. Petaluma had been under smallpox quarantine for a month. Our effort was among the first public gatherings after the quarantine was lifted.

Our tent services opened Thursday evening, August 13, with an attentive crowd. On our arrival in San Francisco, a letter from Sister White was awaiting us with counsel about our manner of labor in California. In New England, Elder Bourdeau and I had been very careful to make ends meet, but her counsel now was "You cannot labor in California as you did in New England. Such strict economy would be considered 'pennywise' by the Californians. Things are managed there on a more liberal scale. You will have to meet them in the same liberal spirit."

The smallest coin then used in California was ten cents. When people saw our tracts at one and two cents each, they asked, "Do you expect to sell these? There are no cents in circulation here." We replied, "Then we can give them away."

We had packages of various pamphlets totaling 500 pages which we priced at 50 cents each. Handing us a dollar one man said, "A dollar is cheap enough." Others followed his example, and within a few minutes our stand was completely cleared of tracts. Before the meetings closed we had sold our fourth shipment of books from Elder White who commented, "You are selling more books there than all our tent companies east of the Rockies." Our meetings in Petaluma closed on Sunday night, October 18. Although there was opposition from the ministers of the town, and even Mr. Wolf turned against us, twenty persons accepted the truth.

At the close of one of the services, three men from Windsor, 25 miles north, urged us to hold our next series there, so on November 4, we began in a free meeting-house in their little country village. Although the opposition we met in Petaluma followed us here, about a dozen accepted the message, among them Dr. Krieschbaum and Madam Parrot, a French lady graduate from a medical college in Geneva.

It was while Abram LaRue, our first missionary to China, was chopping wood for one of our Windsor brethren that he read our publications, attended meetings, and was baptized. J. F. Wood of Walla Walla, Washington, had moved to California to "get rid of the Sabbath" urged upon him by an Adventist neighbor. He rented a farm near Windsor and, strangely enough, attended our meetings. Here he accepted the Sabbath and later returned with his family to Walla Walla where he held meetings and organized a church.

Mr. Lyttaker, a Petaluma blacksmith, accepted the message and traded his home for forty acres west of Santa Rosa where he moved and set up shop. Many teamsters from Santa Rosa passed his place daily, and gave him more business than ever before. Soon he sent an earnest request for us to hold meetings, and secured the Blakely schoolhouse in his neighborhood. Because this small building could not accommodate the increasing audience, we moved to a larger schoolhouse at Piner for March and April meetings.

The people showed great interest despite heavy rains and bad roads. But the creek in the valley swelled so high that it washed away bridges or covered them with water. To meet this problem, we conducted meetings on both sides of the creek, speaking at Lyttakers every other day, and at the schoolhouse every evening. We baptized eleven, and the same day voted a temporary conference organization with Elder Bourdeau as president, Robert Morton as secretary, and myself as treasurer. One of the brethren then came forward and laid a $5 gold-piece on the desk saying, "What is the use of having a treasurer unless you have money in the treasury?"

While we were at Piner, an evangelist was conducting a revival in a popular church of Santa Rosa. When he learned that some of his members attended our meetings, he came out and challenged us to a two-day debate which we accepted. Such an immense crowd responded, we held it in Mr. Peugh's barn nearby. The Sonoma Democrat reported, "Everything that ran on wheels went out to the second day of the debate." Recognizing the weakness of his own arguments against the Sabbath, the evangelist declared, "Well, I can beat the elder in hollering if in no other way."

After the debate closed, I went into Santa Rosa and found the town all astir. One man commented about the debate, I never saw such a thing! It's like the handle of a jug, all on one side (referring to the Sabbath side of the question)." Doctors, merchants, and even the town dentist hailed me on the street and asked, "Aren't you going to pitch your tent here, and make your next effort in this city?" One doctor went with me and secured a lot on which to erect a tent, then found rooms for us. Lumber for seats and everything else for the tent was furnished without cost. The editor of the Democrat said, "Elder, my paper is open for you to say anything you wish about your meetings." So we decided to erect our tent here and come in on the full tide.

Feeling that we had reached a turning point where we would see more rapid progress in our work, Elder Bourdeau and I had an earnest season of prayer, and that night the Lord gave me an impressive dream. I dreamed that after we had ascended a mountain and were starting down the other side, we were faced with an abrupt rise of rocks fifty feet high and no apparent way around. Then a man appeared and told us to begin the ascent and a pathway to the right would soon appear. We followed his directions only to find a perpendicular wall to our left and a deep chasm to our right. A misty cloud covered our path fifty feet ahead, but as we advanced, the cloud moved away.

Down in the valley we saw a vast company of people boarding long trains of cars. On three sets of tracks, trains extended as far as the eye could see. It was interpreted to us that the resurrection had occurred. I saw Elder and Mrs. White stepping from one car to another and greeting the resurrected saints. As our train swung around, Elder White exclaimed, "Here comes the California train! We are all going to the city!" At this I awoke, thrilled with the thought that this dream was a token of victory in California.

On April 22, 1869, we began a six-week series of tent meetings at Santa Rosa which was well attended. When we presented the Bible doctrine of spiritual gifts, the pastor of the largest church in the city told his people, "The gifts were given only until the Christian church was established." But soon a miracle of healing occurred that upset his theory and brought even more people to our tent.

On April 20, Sister Skinner of the Piner district became seriously ill, and called for Sister Parrot, M.D., to give her medical care. By May 10, Mrs. Skinner was so much better, Dr. Parrot felt she could leave, and planned to spend a few days at our meeting before returning to her home in Windsor. That evening a horse was readied with side-saddle for her to ride to our house. Mrs. Skinner's son Oliver planned to come on another horse and take it back.

The horse Dr. Parrot was to ride was used to ladies, and was considered perfectly gentle and safe, but for some unknown reason, when she mounted him, he began to rear and pitch furiously, not only throwing her off, but falling upon her in such a way that the saddle struck across her arms and chest with such force as to bend the horn out straight. When her friends picked her up and carried her to the house, they feared she was dead. She regained consciousness, but could not speak above a whisper. When someone suggested they send for a doctor, she replied, "No! A doctor can do me no good. Send for the ministers at the tent. If they come and pray, the Lord will heal me."

Just as Elder Bourdeau and I were about to open our evening service, Oliver arrived with Dr. Parrot's request. Thinking it unwise to send our congregation home, we promised to come as early as possible in the morning.

Taking my wife along, we left before dawn with Jackson Ferguson driving his wagon. On arrival we learned that her condition had required four attendants to care for her during the night. She whispered to us, "Anoint me and pray, and the Lord will heal me."

As we prayed, commending her to the Great Physician, my wife anointed her. Soon Dr. Parrot began to pray in a loud voice, clapped her hands and said, "I am healed." She arose, dressed herself, and walked to another room to see Mrs. Skinner, after which she helped get dinner. She rode in a chair on a lumber wagon into Santa Rosa where she attended the evening service free from all pain. Oliver Skinner, who called himself an infidel, was astonished and became a good witness to many inquirers.

But we were not left with simply one demonstration of the Lord's willingness to heal. Mr. Ferguson's sister-in-law, a bedfast invalid and unable to attend meetings, requested us to come to her house and present some of the things we were teaching at the tent. So we hung our charts beside her bed and gave her a synopsis of our meetings, returning once a week throughout the month of May.

On May 26, Father Ferguson was to be baptized in Santa Rosa Creek, about 200 feet from their door. Both of the sons were there with their families. The invalid daughter-in-law said, "I, too, want to be baptized. The Lord who has heard my prayers and forgiven my sins will give me strength to be baptized."

She was dressed for the occasion, placed in a chair in a wagon which was then driven into the water. Elder Bourdeau took one side of the chair and I the other and carried her to the proper depth. As we raised her from the water she shouted, "Glory!" her face radiant with the light of heaven. She then walked to the wagon and got in without assistance. She made her own change of clothing at her house, declared herself free from illness and prepared dinner for the company.

Great was the astonishment of the people on Sabbath, to see this sister come to the meeting in a lumber wagon, sit on hard board seats all through the services, return to the evening meeting, then home again in that uncomfortable wagon.

We next moved our tent to Healdsburg, yet at the same time continued meetings at Piner. Here opposition came from an unexpected source—the parents and in-laws of some of our converts. Since Jackson Ferguson was one of the trustees of the Monroe schoolhouse, and had obtained a favorable reply from a second trustee, he announced a meeting there for the next Sabbath. As I rode to my appointment early Sabbath morning, I passed a man going to Santa Rosa with a load of wood. He shouted, "Elder, you are going to have trouble today! Old Mr. Morton will not let you in the schoolhouse. I am going with my load of wood but will stop and see how it all comes out."

When I arrived at ten o'clock, I tied my horse behind the building and walked in. Only the women were inside. The men were all out in the street talking with Mr. Morton who was so excited he did not see me enter. He said, "Loughborough shall not go into that house today!"

"But he is in there already," one of the men laughed.

Hearing this, Morton rushed in, seized me by the arm and shouted, "Get out of this house, you liar, you thief, you blasphemer!" He pulled me to the door, and with a push sent me into the street.

"What do you mean by these charges?" I asked the enraged man.

He replied, "You lied in saying that the wicked will be burned up root and branch." I calmly responded, "Those are the words of Mal. 4:1"

Then he said, "You are a thief; you stole my son. You are a blasphemer in teaching that the soul is not immortal!"

When I made reference to a few scriptures, he began to swing his cane over my head as though he would strike me and yelled, "You are Mormons!"

One of the men standing by began to pull off his coat saying, "Elder, let me pitch into that man. He shall not abuse you so."

"Just keep your coat on," I said. "He's really helping us more than he's hurting us."

Then turning to Morton I asked, "How is it that I am turned out of the house when I had the consent of two-thirds of the trustees?"

He replied, "I am one of the trustees, but I have changed my mind."

Adjoining the school grounds was a grove of live oaks, one of which had wide-spreading branches providing sixty feet of shade. Here under this tree our people gathered and sat upon the grass for the Sabbath services. The opposition of Mr. Morton made possible a building of our own. The owner of the two lots upon which the tent had been pitched deeded us the ground and also gave $500. Then many promised cash donations, and a contractor offered to superintend the erection of the building.

Since the Piner schoolhouse had always been open for religious services, we announced the next Sabbath meeting to be held there, unaware of new opposition from Mr. Peugh, father of two recent converts. Peugh now shared Morton's sentiments that we were Mormons.

After assisting Elder Bourdeau with the Healdsburg meetings during the week, I prepared for the Sabbath service at the Piner schoolhouse. My wife said, "I am deeply impressed that there is trouble ahead. I'm going with you tomorrow."

Sabbath morning, June 19, we went with our horse and buggy to Mrs.

Skinner's arriving at 7 a.m. Here we learned that Mr. Peugh had nailed shut the windows and doors of the schoolhouse saying, "Loughborough shall not enter this place again." He had also sharpened a huge butcher knife and prepared a long club to waylay me and kill me. After breakfast we saw him armed with knife and club, pass the house taking the road along which we had just come from Healdsburg. Of course, he did not expect us until about meeting time. I said to Mrs. Skinner, "I hope he will have a good time up the road waiting for me."

Chapter 12

A Testimony Perfectly Timed

As Oliver Skinner started off to open the schoolhouse, he slipped a revolver into his pocket saying, "If Peugh puts Loughborough out of that schoolhouse today, he will do it over my dead body."

At our meeting I spoke from Philippians 3:14: "I press toward the mark for the prize of the high calling in Christ Jesus." Near the close of my sermon, Mr. Peugh came into the yard. He saw that something had gone wrong with his plans. I announced a meeting there for the next Sabbath, then closed the service. The men then formed a cordon around the angry man until we had gotten off the grounds.

The next week, Mr. Peugh went before the grand jury to make a complaint against me, and to request that my preaching be stopped. But the judge, having learned of his threat on my life and his unlawful closing of the schoolhouse said, "Mr. Peugh, go home and keep quiet, for by your own course you have laid yourself liable to prosecution."

While at Healdsburg on July 6, I was handed a copy of the California Christian Advocate which reported our meetings, comparing them with the Millerite movement of 1844. The editor had written, "Back then they harangued the crowds that came out to hear on prophecy. Finally, they set a time for the Lord to come, and on the appointed day, in their ascension robes, went into graveyards or climbed upon housetops.… This movement in Healdsburg is of the same character. The men conducting the meeting neither preach nor pray.… They have books to sell on Daniel and Revelation. The people need not fear that anything permanent will result from this excitement."

A few weeks later while I was sitting in the tent, the mail stage halted in front, and the driver said, "Here's a letter for you folks." It was addressed "To the Elders at the Tent in Healdsburg, California." The letter read: "Excuse me for addressing you as The Elders at the Tent, for I do not know your names. You probably saw the article in the recent number of the California Christian Advocate reporting your tent meetings in Healdsburg. In that article it said you had books to sell treating on the book of Revelation. For 20 years I have been studying that book, and I have written to New York, Philadelphia, and other places to get some treatise explaining it, but have failed. I wish you would forward to me by Wells Fargo Express one of the books that you are selling on Revelation. Send it C.O.D., and I will remit the pay and be greatly obliged to you. William Hunt, Gold Hill, Nevada."

Here we had a verification of the scripture, "they can do nothing against the truth, but for the truth." The thrust in the paper against us had made a call for the truth. I made up a package of books for Mr. Hunt and sent them by mail to save expense. Then I wrote him a lengthy letter explaining about the editor's slur against Adventists, and telling him of our people and what we were doing. I mentioned other of our books and our weekly paper *The Advent Review and Sabbath Herald*.

On August 1, when the Wells Fargo agent again handed me a letter from Gold Hill, Nevada, he added, "There's a money package for you at the office, but I could not bring it until you sign for it."

Mr. Hunt wrote that he had read through the entire package of material, and was reading it the second time. He was thankful he had found so much light and said he believed it all. He added, "I don't want to lose your whereabouts, so when you leave Healdsburg be sure to give me your post office address." He ordered the *Review* for a year, and also the other books I mentioned. "I send you by Wells Fargo, $20." he wrote. "Take out the pay for the books, and put the rest in your pocket for yourself."

I sent him the books he requested, and told him I did not want to keep the money for myself. Soon he responded with another $20 to apply toward tent meeting expense. The correspondence continued until we had sent him a copy of everything the denomination published, including a set of the Testimonies. In response he sent a third $20, and told us he believed everything we taught and was shaping his affairs to keep the Sabbath. By this time we knew we need not be alarmed at a little reproach against us.

On September 3, legal papers were signed in Santa Rosa completing the organization of a society to hold church property. The way was then opened to erect a church building in that city—the first Seventh-day Adventist meetinghouse erected west of the Rocky Mountains. We then moved our tent seven miles west of Sebastopol.

October 11, was set as the day to lay the foundation of the new Santa Rosa church. When my wife and I arrived at the time appointed, we were astonished to find the foundation already laid with joists in place for the floor. The brethren explained, "We got here early, so thought we might as well go to work as stand around waiting for 9 o'clocks to come." I replied, "Alright! But if my eyes do not deceive me, the building you've started is more than fifty feet long. Didn't we vote 30 x 50?"

Mr. Walker, the head builder, replied, "When we measured of 50 feet, we decided it would be too small, so we took the liberty to add another 10 and stand the expense."

"California liberality!" I laughed.

By early November the building was enclosed. We seated it temporarily with benches from the tent, and held our first meeting November 21, with Elder Bourdeau speaking on the text, "I was glad when they said, Let us go into the house of the Lord." Ps.122:1 Some feared our church was built too large, yet it was filled to capacity the first day. At the close of the service, four candidates were baptized in Santa Rosa Creek. Bro. Hewitt let us live in one of his houses, and on November 26, our daughter Patience was born.

April 8–10, 1871, a session of our State Association was held in Santa Rosa. Merritt Kellogg, who had just moved here, was with us. This was timely, for Elder Bourdeau planned to return East to labor for the French people. To save expense, we had lived together as one family since our arrival in San Francisco. As we did final bookkeeping, a surprise balance awaited us. Our total fares from New York were met to the very penny by our total profit from the sale of books.

Beginning May 5, Merritt Kellogg and I held tent meetings at Bloomfield. The interest and attendance was splendid until June 9, when a smallpox epidemic broke out. Dr. Kellogg then used his medical skill in the homes of the afflicted ones. His kindness and successful treatment created a very favorable impression and an interest in our health message. By June 25, the danger was over and we continued our meetings.

While holding a second series of meetings in Bloomfield during December, I noticed a stranger in the audience paying very close attention. Afterwards, one of the members introduced him saying, "Here is a man from Nevada who is staying at our lodging house and wishes to speak with you."

"And his name is William Hunt," I said, "with whom I have been corresponding since July 1869."

"I am the man," responded the stranger. "I have come to spend a few days here before leaving the United States."

He stayed at Bloomfield five days, and before leaving asked for a set of charts, and any books he might not already have. He said, "I'm going to sail for New Zealand, and if things do not open up there, I shall go to the diamond mines of South Africa."[1]

After paying for the charts, he handed me a ten-dollar gold piece as a present, saying, "I shall probably never see you again, but you will hear from me after a while. I shall, by the Lord's help, ever faithfully obey the truth."

During the winter of 1870–71, Elder Miles Grant, a First-day Adventist minister from New England, came to San Francisco and raised a great interest in prophecy. Later in the spring, a revivalist from the East held successful tent meetings here. We felt it would be wise to erect our tent in the city just after these meetings closed. So on June 14, our meetings opened on Market St. with every seat filled. On the second evening, Elder M. E. Cornell arrived from the East to assist me. We continued our meetings until July 27, when the northwest trade winds became so cold we accepted an offer to meet in the Baptist Church on Sixth Street.

An experience came to us in January, 1872, which served to confirm the faith of that young church in the spirit of prophecy. Elder Cornell persisted in an independent course which I felt would bring reproach upon himself and upon the cause. Innocent as it seemed, he conducted himself

---

1   William Hunt did go to the diamond fields at Kimberly, and with literature introduced S.D.A. teachings into South Africa

injudiciously with a lady of the congregation, showing partiality which aroused comment among the enemies of the faith. Although far from the borders of immorality, I reasoned with him that he should shun every appearance of evil. He said it was nobody's business, and that he could walk the streets with whomever he pleased. The older church members saw the evil of his waywardness and were ready to subject him to censure, but the younger ones sided with him.

Thus the matter stood on Sabbath, January 27, when it was decided than an investigation must be made and action taken. To all appearances a division in the church was inevitable. A meeting was appointed for 9 a.m. Sunday morning. I spent much of the night in prayer. On the morning of the 28th, as I started out for the meeting, I met my fellow-laborer on the sidewalk, near my boarding place, weeping. He said, "Brother Loughborough, I am not going to that meeting today."

"Not going to the meeting?" I asked in astonishment. "Why, that meeting relates to your case!"

"I know," he said, "but I am all wrong. You are right in the position you have taken in reference to me. Here is a letter of confession I have written to the church. It is better that you read it to them, and better for those who might sympathize with me if I were not there."

"But what has happened to make such a great change since yesterday?" I inquired.

He explained, "I went to the post office last night after the Sabbath, and received a letter from Sister White," he said handing me the letter. "Tell the church I accept it as a testimony from God, and that I repent."

The letter read, "I was shown, Brother Cornell, that you should be very circumspect in your deportment and in your words; you are watched by enemies. You have great weakness for a man that is as strong to move the crowd as you are. Separated from your wife as you are, suspicion and jealousy will frame falsehood if you give no occasion; but if you are careless, you will bring a reproach upon the cause of God which would not soon be wiped away. Satan is tempting you to make a foolish man of yourself. Now is your opportunity to show yourself a man, to accept the grace of God by your patience, your fortitude and courage. Be careful how you are enticed to make woman your confidants, or to allow them to make you their confidant. Keep aloof from the society of women as much as you can; you will be in danger."

But we must go back. This counsel came to Sister White in a vision shown her on *December* 10, 1871, while traveling in Vermont. She began to write out the part relating to Elder Cornell on *December* 27, but she did not complete it at that time. Early on the morning of January 18, 1872, she awoke with the impression, "Write out immediately the testimony for California and get it in the very next mail. It is needed." Then the impression came a second time. She arose quickly and completed the letter. Before breakfast she handed it to her son Willie saying, "Take the letter to the post office, but do not put it in the drop. Hand it to the postmaster, and have him be sure to put it in the mail bag that goes out this morning."

At that time it required nine days for overland mail between Michigan and California. Had the letter arrived a day later, there would doubtless have been a sad rupture in the church. Had it come several days earlier, the church would not so readily have seen its force. Our members in San Francisco saw at once that no person on the west coast could have communicated that information to Mrs. White in time for her to write that letter, for the state of things which had developed did not then exist. The perfect timing of the counsel confirmed the church in the Spirit of Prophecy.

On April 25–28, 1872, we held a California State Meeting at Santa Rosa. Sensing a debt of gratitude to the General Conference, a fund of $2,000 was raised for a mutual obligation fund, and sent to Battle Creek together with an invitation for Elder and Mrs. White to spend the winter of 1872–73 with us. As we studied the needs of the field, it was agreed that Elder Cornell and I should hold the next tent meetings at Woodland, twelve miles from Sacramento.

Chapter 13

With the Whites Again

We arrived in Woodland May 21, secured lodging with Judge Johnson, and the next day erected our tent opposite the courthouse and announced a meeting for that evening. Our coming so suddenly into town caused quite an excitement and crowded our tent to overflowing.

We did not know that William Saunders, editor of a county paper, had attended a full series of lectures at Charlotte, Michigan, in 1862, and almost accepted the message. He advised the people both privately and through the Yolo County paper to attend the meetings. Leading men of the city came—the deputy sheriff, the county treasurer, the bank cashier, the court crier, and others. On the third Sunday a special train came from Knight's Landing with a load to attend the meeting. Since the pastors of the two main churches were both away on business, we had no opposition until the people had an opportunity to study for themselves.

Not only were books taken freely by the people, but on the ninth evening the court crier arose and said, "These men are talking about things in which we are deeply interested. They have made no call for help but we wish to do something. I am going to take a collection, and I want you to dig deep into your pockets." Then he passed around his tall, white beaver hat and collected $51.55. After the presentation of the Seal of God and the Mark of the Beast, nearly forty people took their stand for the Sabbath. The court crier arose again. "I am not satisfied with our collection last Sunday. Although these ministers shake their heads, I'm going to take another." Around went the beaver hat for an additional $41.10.

One afternoon the heavens became black, distant thunder rumbled, and rain began about the time of the evening meeting. But so great was the interest, 300 came out. No uneasiness was manifested because of the heavy rain upon the canvas, or anxiety about how they would get home through the darkness, mud, and rain.

When we learned that Elder and Mrs. White were coming in September, and that they suggested a camp meeting, we closed our meetings at Woodland on September 15. The camp meeting was held in a grove at Windsor September 30 to October 3. Surrounding the main tent were 36 camping tents, and what a variety they were! Although some were regular tents, others were hastily erected frames with sheets or rugs thrown over them, and some were rough board shanties. A man who did not hear of the meeting until the night before, piled fence rails between stakes driven close together, then used a shawl for a door. Since the weather was fair and dry, no one suffered. Of the 16 messages given at this meeting, 13 were delivered by Elder or Mrs. White. Those attending from Woodland wished that the tent be pitched there again and the Whites speak to them, so we held a second series October 15 to November 4.

At the close of our San Francisco effort in November, Elder Cornell returned to Woodland to take charge of erecting a house of worship and to follow up the interest. While the church was under construction, we were given free use of the courthouse. From December 5, 1872, until February 20, 1873, the Whites made their home at my house in Santa Rosa, holding meetings with the different companies in Sonoma County. On February 16, 1873, they assisted in the organization of the California State Conference at our meeting hall in Bloomfield. Seven churches were voted into the conference, and the number of Sabbath-keepers reported as 238.

It was here that three professed Sabbath-keepers publicly objected to the chairman of the meeting appointing the committees on nominations, credentials, and resolutions—a plan which had been followed for many years. One of the men said, "I think we ought to conduct business on the floor, just like a caucus or a political meeting. Let everyone ballot to see who gets the highest number of votes." Another said, "If you are going to have a committee, I don't believe in that because it is a one-man power." Then a testimony came from Sister White that this was not the way to proceed, but that when we select committees, we should carefully and prayerfully consider what is needed, and the qualifications of persons, then after seeking the counsel of the brethren, begin to suggest the names.

But these men in a turbulent manner pressed their views, hardly giving opportunity for Elder or Mrs. White to say anything. In their remarks these men often said that they did not believe in "one-man power." Finally, Elder White obtained the floor and calmly said to the leader of the trio, "I see you do not believe in one-man power unless you can be that one man."

On March 13, I began meetings in the Red Banks schoolhouse six miles west of Red Bluff.

Mr. Wilkins, a bookkeeper in a large mercantile establishment and an infidel, was afflicted with tuberculosis. A few weeks earlier his mother, Mrs. Horne who lived in Baltimore and was greatly concerned about his health, came to visit him. On the way from Chicago to Sacramento, she rode in the same car with the Whites. Sister White had given her copies of health papers and also some advice on how to care for her son. The son read the papers, put the principles into practice, and was receiving great benefit. When he saw the notice of my meetings in the courthouse he said, "Mother, I would not wonder if that man is one of Mrs. White's people. I am going to this meeting to see, and if he is one of her faith, I am going to ask him home with me." My visits with that family were frequent, and they attended all the meetings in the courthouse.

On April 13, it was my privilege to baptize five candidates in the Sacramento River three miles south of Red Bluff. Among them were Mother Horne and her son, Mr. Wilkins. To some of our opponents who had accused us of dividing families, Mr. Wilkins replied, "Not much division here. My mother was a Methodist, my wife a Baptist, and I was an infidel. There was nothing I delighted in more than to get them into a religious argument. Before the meetings our family was three, but now we are one in the faith."

At the spring council of the California Conference, 1873, it was planned to hold tent meetings in the Napa Valley during the summer, the first to be held at Napa City, and the second in St. Helena. These were to be followed by a fall camp-meeting at Yountville, midway between Napa and St. Helena. With a new sixty-foot circular tent we began our effort in Napa, May 24, and continued until July 27. Forty decided to obey the truth, and the old schoolhouse was obtained for Sabbath services.

On July 30, we began meetings in St. Helena and continued until September 14. On the last two days there was a debate on the Sabbath question between Elder Cornell and Prof. Martin of Woodland. At its close Elder McCorkle, a local pastor, pled for a donation for Martin's travel expenses. The audience wanted to take a collection and divide it between the debaters, but Elder McCorkle would not agree to this. He said, "Since no decision has been made upon the debate, I suggest we put a hat on each side of the table, and let the audience, as they pass out, put into the hat of either party their contribution of how they view the case." Our tentmaster reported that the professor's hat contained about $2.50, while in Elder Cornell's hat was nearly $30.

Our camp-meeting at Yountville opened September 17. Besides our sixty-foot tent there were 53 other tents. Our grounds were laid out in city style with Present Truth Street, Law and Order Street, Santa Rosa Street, Healdsburg Street, Petaluma Avenue, etc. (The Yolo Democrat reported, "The most perfect order and harmony prevailed throughout. We never before saw such a large crowd of happy and devoted people. There was no excitement, but a great degree of earnest zeal was manifested throughout the meetings." September 26, 1873). During one social meeting 117 testimonies were given in 53 minutes. All right to the point.

The Yountville camp-meeting exerted a powerful influence in giving stability to the work in California. It was here that M. J. Church of Fresno accepted the message and opened the way for its introduction into that part of the country. In one of the meetings he arose and said, "I am constructing an irrigation canal from King's River. I have forty men in my employ, but from this time on that work shall all stop on the Lord's Sabbath." After camp meeting we moved to Woodland thinking a dryer climate would be better for my wife who was then afflicted with tuberculosis.

In 1873, Sister Willis of Santa Rosa had moved to Oakland and was anxious for something to be done there. Brother Cronkite moved his shoe-shop to Oakland, and Brother Tay and family accepted the truth. These persons all requested meetings for Oakland, so I held the first meeting there October 25, 26 in a hall at 1055 Broadway.

On November 12, Sister L. M. Hall, with two of the Walling girls from Colorado, who were to live in Elder White's family, came to Santa Rosa and occupied my house. On *December* 28, Elder and Mrs. White arrived from Colorado, and during that winter labored among the different companies in California. At Napa we were rapidly completing our church and preparing for its dedication on April 4. The sermon was given by Elder White, and in the afternoon his wife spoke with great freedom to a full audience.[1]

The few believers at Walla Walla, Washington had pled with the General Conference for a worker. At the Yountville camp-meeting our people voted to pay the expense of a minister to Walla Walla if they would permit him to labor two or three months in California on his way. In response, Elder I. D. VanHorn and his wife came to Colorado to accompany the Whites to California. On January 2, 1874, Elder VanHorn went with me to Napa where we held meetings over the weekend, then on to St. Helena and Woodland. Here I received word of deep interest in Canright's meetings at Watsonville, but that difficulty with his throat demanded he have rest and help. He wished me to come to help him immediately. I was in Watsonville January 22 to February 2, when I received a telegram calling me to return at once to Woodland as my wife's lung trouble was worse. As Elder Canright had recovered enough to continue, I left immediately for home.

At Watsonville I met Brother Healey and his sister who had embraced the truth in Minnesota, and had just come to California.

Elder VanHorn took the steamer for Portland, Oregon, en route to Walla Walla, arriving there April 23, 1874. He pitched his new sixty-foot tent in the southeastern part of town on land owned by Charlie Cabot. Although Cabot was a Catholic, he donated the lot upon which the tent had been pitched for the erection of a church. He did all he could to advance the cause, accepted the message, and willed to the church $60,000.

---

1   Senator Nathan Coombs donated a lot on the corner of Church and 2nd Streets, and a church building was erected by the winter of 1873–74. The original building still stands.

Within sight of the tent stood a fort and a garrison of soldiers, among whom was Alonzo T. Jones, an Ohio boy. While the other soldiers spent their free time playing cards and other useless habits, Jones studied history books. As the tent was being erected, Jones and others became curious and stopped by. "What is this?—a show?" they asked. "Yes," replied Elder VanHorn. "Come in and I will tell you what we are going to show." He unrolled a prophetic chart and began to go over the symbols of Babylon, Medo-Persia, Greece, etc., referring to historical facts. To VanHorn's exposition Jones would give additional facts, showing his familiarity with those ancient kingdoms. Jones came to the meetings, listened intently, and then joined the Seventh-day Adventists.

In the *Review* of April 21, 1874, Elder White proposed that a paper (*Signs of the Times*) be published on the Pacific Coast. At that time we had planned to hold meetings in Cloverdale, Medocino County, and had already shipped the sixty-foot tent. When Elder and Mrs. White came to visit the families of Sister Willis and Brother Tay, Sister White said to her husband, "This is just the place I saw we should locate the paper." That being the case, it seemed of greatest importance to present the truth in Oakland. Elder White immediately decided to move his household effects here from Santa Rosa. As they prayed over the matter, they were so impressed that the tent meetings should be held here, they could not sleep. Elder White started for Alexander Valley near Healdsburg, fording the Russian River to intercept the team that was to take the tent to Cloverdale. He was just in time, and the tent was put on the train for Oakland. The tent was erected on a beautiful lot in April, and meetings conducted by Elders Canright and Cornell.

The erecting of the tent in Oakland proved to be the order of the Lord, for soon after the meetings opened, the great temperance "local option" movement came on. For ten day's use of our tent they gave us $100 in gold. On May 29, we erected a new sixty-foot tent in East Oakland where there was another week of temperance meetings, and the society paid us $50 for the use of the tent. The giving of our influence and votes to the "local option" movement brought about a strong bond of sympathy for us by those who opposed the sale of liquor. During the temperance rally in Oakland, the people had well learned the way to our tents, and our efforts in the meetings that followed were a success in both tents which were two miles apart.

Sunday, June 14, was a delightful day for a baptism at the water's edge of beautiful Lake Merritt. Upon a bluff 30 feet above the shore were gathered from 1,500 to 2,000 people, while many little boats rode upon the water. Before the baptism, Elder White gave a short, earnest and convincing sermon upon the law and baptism. All listened with the greatest respect, after which 23 were baptized.

How well I remember the day in Oakland when we met in Elder Canright's room, and *Signs*, volume 1, number 1 was brought in sheets from the press and laid upon the floor. Elder and Mrs. White, Elder and Mrs. Canright, and myself bowed in prayer and asked God's blessing upon the "new paper." It was with trembling, anxiety, and yet with faith in God that Elder White moved out in this enterprise. Time has shown that it was just what was needed. Great is the good already accomplished by this instrumentality.

Although we wanted to present the message in San Jose, we had not seen the way clear. But now the temperance people asked for one of our tents to hold meetings there, gave us $100, and paid all expenses for moving and erecting it. When their meetings closed June 27, we secured the use of the same ground, and on July 2 opened with a message by Elder Canright. He and Elder Cornell continued there, and over 30 were baptized.

As the summer heat at Woodland was too great for my wife's feeble condition, we sold our house at Santa Rosa and moved to St. Helena. On September 24, we pitched our two sixty-foot tents side by side with a connecting canvas, on the Yountville campground. We were favored in having Elder George I. Butler, a member of the General Conference committee, with us for the first time. Since my wife was anxious to enjoy the meetings and felt it might be her last opportunity, we arranged a tent for her and her sister just behind the meeting tent. Here she could lie upon her bed and still hear the preaching.

On October 11, we told the people that the General Conference wished us to raise $4,000 for sustaining the *Signs of the Times*. The presence of God came into the meeting, and in a few minutes time, with no urging, there was pledged $19,414. We had planned to call that afternoon for a camp-meeting fund of $500, but in the afternoon meeting we told them that they had pledged so liberally in the morning, we did not feel free to ask them to pledge any more. Brother T. M. Chapman said, "Try us on it, and see if we will not raise a tent and camp-meeting fund." He started it off with $50, and in a short time there were pledges of $1,616. This was the third and largest camp-meeting ever held in California. On the last day, 49 were baptized in Napa Creek which ran by the side of the camp, among them Knud Brorsen who became a pioneer worker in Norway.

Wesley Diggins of San Francisco made an earnest request that the double tent be erected in his city. We secured a lot on Golden Gate Ave., and opened meetings October 16. Elder Butler took part until November 1, when he and Elder Cornell returned to Michigan. Attendance was between 800 and 1,200 nightly.

My labors were associated more or less with the Whites until February, when the failing health of my companion called for my attention at home in St. Helena. I spoke to the company there on Sabbaths until she peacefully passed away on March 24. She sleeps quietly in the St. Helena cemetery.

On April 14, the leading members of the San Francisco church met at the home of Sister J. L. James, and Sister White related to us what had been shown her in vision. She stated that San Francisco would always be a mission field, and urged upon us the importance of erecting a house of worship. It would look to that poor church like a move in the dark, but if they moved out as the providence of God opened the way, the cost would be entirely met. Knowing as I did the financial condition of these members, to build a church 35 x 80, where a lot alone cost $6,000, looked indeed like a "leap in the dark."

But we found a lot on Laguna Street for $4,000. Then one sister promised $1,000 if she could sell her place, and within two weeks she sold it for $1,000 above the price she had valued it. A brother who could not see how a church could be built said, "If the Lord says it must be done, He will open the way. Soon he received $20,000 from an estate settlement and gave $1,000. The church was erected for $14,000, including the price of the lot, over half of which was paid for before it was finished. Then the school district rented the lower rooms at $75 a month for the next two years."

At the Yountville camp-meeting in 1877, the songs of the birds at dawn in our beautiful grove led many of the people to report their awakening thoughts at the early morning meetings. This was the first camp-meeting in which we used an organ in our song service. J. Edson White secured the free use of a good organ from a San Francisco dealer by permitting the dealer to hang a printed card with his name and address in view of the audience. Since there were a few persons who objected to the use of instrumental music in public worship, I read the 150th Psalm in the first early meeting. "Praise Him with the sound of the trumpet; praise Him with the Psaltery and harp; praise Him with the timbrel and pipe; praise Him with stringed instruments and ..." as I came to the next word, I slowly spelled out "O-R-G-A-N-S," then remarked, "Why that is just the word that is on the back of that box, and in our very next meeting today we are going to have the organ out and praise the Lord with it, just as He has told us to do."

As the meeting closed, our good Scotch Sister Rowland remarked, "I am like the Scotchman who said he believed in praising the Lord with all his might." However, we began that day to use the organ, which made a decided improvement in the song service. In the next morning meeting, I related my thoughts on Sister Rowland's "praising the Lord with all his might." I said, "It takes just an organ to do that. The mind must be on the music; the eyes must be on the notes; the feet must work the pedals; the fingers must touch the keys; and the voice must sing the song of praise; so you have a person praising the Lord with all his might."

As the meeting closed, Sister Rowland said with a smile, "Well, I will come up with you yet." In the next early meeting, she was the first one to speak. "Brethren and sisters, what do you suppose were my first thoughts when I awoke this morning? It was the scripture 'Let everything that hath breath praise the Lord.' My next thought was, 'Why then don't you praise the Lord with things that you can make breathe?'" We had no opposition to instrumental music after this.

The camp-meeting was a decided success, and we witnessed an impressive baptism. Among the candidates were some who had come long distances of 300 miles from the north, and others the same distance from the south.

The State Sabbath School Association was organized with J. E. White as president. It was about this time that we first began to use a blackboard to illustrate subjects for Sabbath schools, and Mary White, the wife of W. C. White, handled the matter with zeal and efficiency.

In the North Pacific, Elders I. D. VanHorn and A. T. Jones spent the summer in tent meetings in East Portland. Soon after our California camp-meetings, the General Conference requested Elder VanHorn and me to spend a few weeks organizing the work in that field. Since there was no railroad from California to Oregon, I made the trip to Portland by steamer then, in company with VanHorn, on to Walla Walla.

The trip was a real contrast to present-day travel. We left Portland by boat at 5 a.m. Monday, and sailed to the Cascades.

Then all the freight was carried on men's shoulders to a train that went three miles on the north side of the river around the Cascades to the old block fort of General Grant's times. There we waited until 4 p.m. while the freight was carried to a second steamer. At 11 p.m. we reached the Dalles where we boarded another train which took us around the Dalles to Celio. At 4 a.m. all the freight was transferred to another steamer taking us to Walula where we spent the night. At 9 a.m. Wednesday, we took passage on Dr. Baker's railroad reaching Walla Walla after 55 hours from Portland. Elder VanHorn and I spent November visiting believers in Upper Columbia and Northwest Oregon.

In the summer of 1877, two families from Santa Rosa moved to St. Clair, Churchill County, Nevada, and later placed a call for me to come. I arrived at Wadsworth Station February 1, 1878, and was met by Jackson Ferguson who took me 35 miles across the desert to St. Clair, passing only one residence on the way. St. Clair is on the Carson River about six miles above the sink, on the edge of the Great American Desert. It is 5 miles from "Rag Town," were the immigrants stopped on Carson River for a few days to change their much-worn garments for better clothing before entering the settlements.

During February we held meetings in the Churchill County Institute, the only school building in the county. The whole community turned out and listened with great interest. In addition to those who had moved here from California, eight covenanted to keep all the commandments. When the question arose about my travel expenses and four weeks of labor, a non-member arose and said, "The way to raise this is to go down into our pockets and hand out the money." Then he laid a $20 gold piece on the desk. Others followed, and in two minutes the sum was more than made up.

On June 10, Sister White, Miss Glover and I took passage from San Francisco on the steamer "Oregon" with a new fifty-foot tent, and an outfit of camping tents for the first Oregon camp-meeting to be held at Salem. It was a taxing, rough sea trip for Sister White, but Captain Conner and the stewardess did all they could for her comfort. On arriving at Portland, we took the train for Salem where we were met by Elder VanHorn.

With a corps of workers, we set up camp in a nice grove of pines near the fairgrounds. The dining tent was so well patronized that it met all the expenses of the camp, including our steamer fare to and from California.

On Sunday the 7th, Sister White spoke to a vast crowd from the music stand in the city park. Her subject, "Parable of the Barren Fig Tree," moved many to tears by the earnest appeals she made. She spoke Tuesday evening in the Methodist Church at the request of the pastor. The choir from the Methodist college rendered excellent singing. On Wednesday, we took passage on the steamer "Idaho" for San Francisco.

In November, 1877, Dr. M. G. Kellogg announced he had secured grounds on the side of Howell Mountain, two and a half miles northeast of St. Helena, for a Rural Health Retreat, located by the side of Crystal Springs. During the winter of 1877–78, a building was erected, and in early 1878 opened for patients.

Chapter 14

Called to England

As early as the spring of 1874, Elder James White began to talk to me about going to England. I hardly knew why he should ask me until I had been in California five years and Elder Cornell explained, "I heard Sister White say in one of her talks, 'If Elder Loughborough is faithful, his labors will yet be called for in England.'"

While I was staying with Elder White in the old "water cure" building on Lafayette Road, one Sabbath afternoon we walked up a mountain where we might have a prayer season. There among the chamise brush we both received clear impressions of duty. My wife's health indicated she was not long for this world. I owned a home in Santa Rosa, but she could not live there because of the occasional fogs. The Lord granted both Elder White and me a rich sense of His presence and light as to duty, that he should solicit money at the eastern camp-meetings for the *Signs of the Times*, and there also came before me a little glimpse into the future.

As I arose from prayer I said to Elder White, "It is all clear about your duty to go East, but the impression came to me as though an audible voice, "Sell your place in Santa Rosa, but do not buy elsewhere. Your labors will be here and there, so you must not be fastened to one place." I immediately put my house up for sale, and in two weeks time received a draft for the sum I desired.

From that time on, Elder White mentioned occasionally that the work should be opened in England, and hinted at my going. In the spring of 1878, he again went to Battle Creek, and from there wrote me to leave California and come to the General Conference to be held there in October, and they would vote that I go to England. I replied with eight reasons why I did not think it advisable to make such a move just then. The most important were these: first, so many enterprises had been begun in the work here that ought to be completed; and second, if I were to go to that field, I ought to have at least a year to study English customs, so as to enter the field understandingly.

Two sentences of White's brief reply swept away my eight reasons for not going that year. He said, "If you stay a year longer to complete what you say is 'begun,' you will find more 'begun' that needs to be finished than you see now. As for the study of English customs and adapting yourself to the work in England, the best place to study those things is right there on the ground where you see the customs for yourself." Still it was not clear in my mind. Having spent ten years in California and witnessed the rise of the work from the first, it was not easy to let go.

After I returned from the Oregon camp-meeting in July, 1878, I spent two busy days at Oakland shipping the tent and fixtures to Reno, Nevada, where I had agreed to hold a tent effort. On the 17th, I took the train for Reno. I showed my ticket to the conductor, then lay down for much needed rest, and with a prayer for light about going to England. After an hour, I was awakened as if someone had shaken me, but there was no one near. Then the thought came vividly to mind, "Put up your household goods for sale and make arrangements to go to England." Although this was contrary to reason, my mind was now at rest.

I wrote to my companion[1] in Oakland telling her to leave the sale of our things to Providence—to put them up for sale, and if they sold, we would take this as evidence it was our duty to go to the General Conference. A day or so later, a brother who was soon to be married bought everything except our books and clothing.

At Reno, with the help of Brother Ferguson, we erected our tent in a central place, and opened the meetings July 21. Up to 500 curious people packed the tent nightly. Sister White, on her way east, stopped over at Reno and on July 30, gave an earnest message on the new birth from 1 John 3. "Behold, what manner of love the Father has bestowed upon us that we should be called the sons of God." Among the number who took

---

1   In 1875, Elder Loughborough married Anna Driscol, secretary treasurer of the Pacific Press. The ceremony was performed by Elder James White.

their stand were two who received their first ideas of our faith at our very first tent meeting in Battle Creek in 1854.[2]

After returning to Oakland, August 21, I spent two days shipping tents, books, etc. for our camp-meeting at Yountville. We had only our conference workers to conduct this meeting, and there was good spiritual interest by our people. On September 5, we bade goodbye to our people in that part of the state, and hurried to the King's County camp-meeting held near Lemoore. I went immediately to Oakland and shipped the tents and supplies to the campground. I arrived at Lemoore in time to preach at 11 a.m. Sabbath, and then on to the campground in the afternoon.

As a result of almost constant labor and travel, I was so wearied that on the morning of September 11, after I had talked about 25 minutes, I fainted away in the pulpit. Elder Healey completed the sermon while the brethren carried me to my tent to recuperate. On Sabbath, 25 candidates were baptized in the irrigation canal not far from the camp. After returning to Oakland, we prepared for our Michigan trip, leaving September 19.

At the General Conference, the advisability of extending the work to Great Britain was considered, and a vote was taken October 14, to send me to that field. After spending a few weeks in New York and Massachusetts, we left South Lancaster for Boston on *December* 10, 1878, expecting to sail for England on the "Homer" of the Warren Line. Mr. O'Hara, the agent, met us at the boat stating that the captain refused to take on any passengers. "But," he continued, "if you consent, we will transfer you free of expense to the 'Nevada' of the Williams and Guion Line, which will sail from New York tomorrow."

In the providence of God, we found ourselves sailing for our English mission from a point about forty yards from the pier from which I sailed June 24, 1868, to enter upon the California mission. Our trip to Liverpool took a little over twelve days. Some days the sea was very rough due to heavy storms which had passed over a few hours before us. On Monday, *December* 30, we arrived safely at Southampton. The steamship "Homer," on which we had expected to sail, was never heard from after leaving Boston Harbor. It is supposed that it capsized in a storm, and went to the bottom of the sea.

---

2   Another convert at Reno was a young black man, Charles M. Kinney, who later attended Healdsburg College and became the first ordained black S.D.A. minister.

We soon found our way to the home of Henry Cavill. This godly family was very happy to see us, and in a few minutes Elder William Ings came in from his missionary work.

The next day we rented a five-room brick house ("Stanley Cottage") for the winter and arranged for Elder Ings to stay with us.

I gave my first sermon in Shirley Hall the first Sunday evening after our arrival in England. Notwithstanding the fog and darkness that caused some to lose their way, we had an audience of 150 persons who gave marked attention to my message from Daniel 2. We gave a number of sermons here, and four individuals accepted the truth.

When spring came, we purchased a sixty-foot tent, erected it in Southampton suburbs, and began meetings May 18. For $40 we purchased a harmonium with excellent tone and used it to add interest to the meetings. About this time Miss Maud Sisley came from Switzerland and united with our company as Bible worker and colporteur. At the close of the meetings, 30 persons signed the covenant to keep all the commandments of God. On August 3, we began services in "Ravenswood" house, having just moved into that spacious building in which there was a large hall.

Six willing souls were immersed at our first baptism at Southampton, February 8, 1880. In June we pitched the tent in Romsey, eight miles from Southampton, and Elder Andrews came from Switzerland to assist as his health would permit. A few accepted the truth in this effort. By July 2, 1881, I had baptized 29 at Southampton.

On the 9th of August our hearts were made sad indeed by receiving a telegram from Battle Creek, telling us of the death of our dear Brother White, and that the funeral would be the next Sabbath (August 13). On the day of the funeral I spoke from Revelation 14:13. I told of Elder White's ardous labors in the past. From these the Lord called him to rest until the Lifegiver shall come.

The first General Conference after the death of Elder White was held at Battle Creek in December 1881. With only a short notice to prepare, I was requested to attend, and to take back with me to England a force of workers who might be trained, and return again to labor in America. The notice was so short that money could not be obtained from America to meet the needs of the work during my absence and to secure my ticket.

We presented the problem to the Lord in prayer and pleaded for Him to open the way.

As we sat at breakfast on the morning of the day that I must secure my ticket, the postman left two letters, one from a man in North England who wrote, "I do not usually pay my tithes until the end of the quarter, and this is only the middle. I have a check for over eight pounds ($40). I am so powerfully impressed that you are in need of this now that I send it to you at once." The other letter was from a Baptist brother who had just entertained me for three days in Manchester while I was attending meetings of the Vegetarian Society and the British Anti-Narcotic League. He said, "I feel impressed that it is my duty to send you five pounds ($25) to aid in your work." Here was over $65 from an unexpected source! We recognized this as a direct answer to prayer.

But there was yet another providence. When I negotiated for a ticket on the steamer "Bristol" of the Great Western Line, there was a delay in its arrival, and the ship "Somerset" was substituted. I went to their office to buy my ticket, but seemed to be forbidden to do so. We prayed over it for another day, then our minds were all turned to the steamer "Rhein" of the North German Lloyd Line, on which I embarked November 16. Although we made our passage during the terrible gales and ocean hurricanes of the last of November, encountering head winds and storms all the way, and were sixteen days making the voyage usually made in eleven, there was no damage to our steamer, and I arrived in Battle Creek on the third day of the conference. The "Somerset" was reported to have used up all her coal in Mid-ocean 24 days later, and drifted under sail to St. Johns, Newfoundland, more than a thousand miles from New York. Had I taken that boat, I would not have arrived until after the conference was over.

On my return to England, I was accompanied by Elder and Mrs. A. A. John, George Drew, Miss Jennie Thayer, and my son and daughter, all of whom entered the work in that field.

On November 9, 1882, we left Southampton for appointments in North England. As we came into Newcastle, our train passed over the river Tyne, which was so far below us that tall-masted sea-going vessels passed under the arches of the bridge. We visited the castle for which this place was named. It was first constructed of wood by Robert, the eldest son of William the Conqueror, in the years 1079–82. The present structure was built of stone by Henry II, in the years 1172–77. It is said to be the most perfect specimen of a Norman castle existing in England. It is now used as a museum. Here are stone idols of our Saxon ancestors, also stone mortars, pestles, and battle-axes.

In the evening we met in the Bible House where I spoke to the Newcastle Vegetarian Society, a large and attentive audience. On the 12th, we arrived at Hull, 21 miles upriver from Grimsby. It was from this point that our ancestors, the Loughboroughs of Leicestershire, set sail for America the latter part of the 18th century. Here I found my friend George Drew doing extensive missionary work on land and on board vessels visiting this port.

We met difficulties in the establishment of our work in Great Britain that were not experienced in America. Those of wealth would not listen to the same man who spoke to the poor. We labored largely with merchants, tradesmen, and laborers. Ignorance prevails among the poorer laborers, the majority of whom were illiterate.

Lords, nobles, and gentry seemed beyond our reach even with colporteurs, for their mansions are surrounded with high walls, with great iron gates locked and barred, and no admission unless you have a note of introduction from some of their own class. In our hope to find truth-loving persons among the wealthy, we saw no way to reach them except by sending them reading matter. Nevertheless, the Lord blessed, and our hearts were cheered to see some souls accepting the light despite perplexities.

In the summer of 1879, when J. N. Andrews came to us from America, he was accompanied by his niece Edith Andrews, and Annie Oyer who were going to Basel, Switzerland, to help in the mission. Since our house was quite small, we arranged lodging for Edith and Annie at a near neighbor's place, Mr. Nippard, with whom Elder Ings had formed a slight acquaintance in his tract distribution work.

Mr. Nippard and his family were friendly with our girls, and as Elder Ings studied the Bible with him, he really drank in the truth, and expressed a desire to do all he could to help it along, although he did not see his way clear to keep the Sabbath. He was the "ship keeper" for the Peninsular and Oriental Steamship Company, which sailed its steamers from Southampton to 80 seaports in the East and West Indies, Africa and Central America.

One day Mr. Nippard told Elder Ings, "I can help you send literature to other ports. Just furnish me with rolls of papers directed to the agent of any port you wish. Enclose a letter asking him to hand them to any one who might be interested. Thus you can place your publications in ports all over the world."

We heeded his advice. At that time we were receiving 1,000 copies of the Signs weekly from America. We would make a roll of Signs, tracts, and papers in other languages, then enclose a letter asking them not only to circulate the tracts, but to inform us if other literature was desired. Although we received replies from South Africa, British Guiana, and other ports, not until 24 years later did we learn how a bundle of the Signs was received at Cape Haitien, Haiti. The agent, not interested in religion, sent the papers to a Baptist minister who gave them to his church members. Among those who received them was a Jamaican named Henry Williams. After reading them, he and his wife began to keep the Sabbath. Though severely persecuted, and at one time had to find safety in the mountains, they remained faithful.

For 20 years they kept the light burning alone. Then in 1904, they attracted the attention of a school principal who felt the third angel's message an answer to his prayers. He wrote a tract telling why he left Catholicism and joined the Adventists. His efforts were very successful, and prepared the way for our mission work on the island.

From January 1, 1879 to October 10, 1883, our workers in England visited 49,140 families and ships, distributed 84,887 papers, and sold nearly $3,000 worth of books. The number of those who embraced the truth was 100.

After arranging the work in England to be managed by others, with my family I sailed from Liverpool for New York, October 10, 1883, on the steamship "City of Rome."

(NOTE: Elder Loughborough spent the next several years visiting camp meetings, and strengthened the work in the North Pacific and California, serving a term as president of the California Conference.)

Chapter 15

European Dreams Come True

During the winter of 1895–96, I dreamed night after night of being in Scandinavia with Elder Lewis Johnson, and attending camp meetings. Now, as I write these things, I do not wish to set you dreaming, but wish to show that the Lord does sometimes give us instruction in this way.

At that time I already had a district assigned me, still I wanted wisdom about it. Also, I had been asked to write a book that would be translated into foreign languages, so I thought perhaps in this way I might go to Scandinavia. But I dreamed of attending camp-meetings, and the first one was held in a building instead of in tents.

"Where are your tents?" I asked in my dream. They replied, "We have a commodious hall in town where we will hold the meetings."

"But where is your lodging house?"

"Oh, it's off in that direction a little ways, and a very good place."

The I dreamed of attending a second camp-meeting, but upon going there found that this was not a camp-meeting either. They explained, "We could not get a place for a camp." We then went into a meeting-house, and found that it was constructed with boards running vertically instead of horizontally. Afterwards, I dreamed of going to a third meeting where we got into a boat, and after twisting around through a narrow channel, reached a wider body of water, then over a strip of land into another lake, and then on to the church where the meeting was held.

When I attended the council meetings during the spring of 1896, and they made arrangements about the different fields, not a word was said about my going to Scandinavia, so I said to myself, "I'll just write that book as well as I can." But soon afterwards came a letter from Elder O. A. Olsen saying, "We want you to go to Scandinavia. Will you do it? Brother Johnson wants you to come, for he thinks they need your testimony. We have sent word to the other members of the committee. What are your impressions?" Well, I wrote him about my dreams, then added, "If the Lord is in it, I am willing to go."

We left New York City on May 27, and arrived at Southampton in seven days. After spending two days in London[1], we proceeded to Gothenburg, Sweden, where we met Sister Wahlberg, and continued on to Eskilstuna, arriving June 9, and was later joined by Elder E. J. Waggoner.

The camp-meetings were advertised to be held at Eskilstuna, Sweden; Fredrikstad, Norway; and Copenhagen, Denmark. When we came to Eskilstuna, I began to look for the camp, but could not see it anywhere. A brother met us, and we asked, "Where is the camp?" He replied, "We have no camp." I remarked, "But it was advertised that way." "Yes," he agreed, "but we have none." When I asked about the lodging place, he pointed, and there it was, just as I had seen it in my dream! I hadn't really thought much about the dream until I reached the meeting hall which looked as natural as though I had seen it before. I said to Elder Johnson,

---

1   Upon his arrival in London by train, Elder Loughborough did not immediately call for his trunk, but went directly to the home of Elder W. A. Spicer. The next day, accompanied by Elder J. O. Corliss, also a guest at the Spicer home, he returned to the railway station to call for his trunk which contained his clothing and a manuscript of a book he was writing. To his bitter disappointment, it could not be found.

The stationmaster asked, "Did you claim your luggage at the train on your arrival?" "I did not think it necessary," the distraught man replied.

"Well, then," said the official, "knowing as you must the customs of the country, and seeing you neglected to care for your luggage at the proper time, it is not strange that it cannot now be located."

On the return trip to the Spicer home, Loughborough appeared depressed, and spent the remainder of the day in near silence except for an occasional remark. "I would not have lost the book manuscript in the trunk for $500.

The following morning, however, he came to the breakfast table in his usual cheerful manner. He explained, "My trunk is safe. I will find it when I arrive in Sweden."

"How do you know?" he was asked. "Was it marked for Sweden?"

"No," he replied. "The only address on it was Topeka, Kansas. But last night I dreamed of landing in Sweden and discovering the trunk there."

Sure enough. When he landed at Gotborg, he found his trunk in plain sight. (adapted from *Review*, February 18, 1937)

"Well, this is all right." He replied, "I was certain that the Lord wanted you over here, for I could not keep from thinking that way."

When we came to Fredrikstad, I asked, "Where is the tent?" They answered, "We could not find any place to pitch it." Then we came to the meetinghouse and I noticed its construction with vertical boards both outside and inside. Upon inquiry I learned that it had been made of logs, but they later boarded it up and down over the logs, just as I had seen in my dream.

While at Fredrikstad, there came a letter from Brother Ottosen saying that we were going to have an outing at Longby, and he wanted Brethren Waggoner, Johnson, and me to go with him in an amphibious boat. The day before the meeting opened in Copenhagen, we made just such a trip in water and over a strip of land twenty rods wide. Now, God may not teach us all by dreams, but He is willing to teach us. His eye is on our pathway, and our ways are in His hands. He will guide us if we put our trust in Him.

During the month of September 1896, Elder Johnson and I met with our believers at Striberg, Orebro, and Grythyttehed. It was a matter of much interest to me to be in Orebro, the very heart of the Advent movement in Sweden in 1843, when the children preached. I met several of those who heard them preach, and talked with men who preached when they were children. I asked one of them, "You preached when you were a boy?" He replied, "Preached! Yes, I had to preach. I had no devising in the matter. A power came upon me, and I said what I was compelled to say."

One told us of a little three-year old girl who thus preached a short distance from Orebro. There were many of five or six years who preached. I went into the old Orebro prison where Ole Boquist and Erik Walbom were imprisoned for preaching the doctrines. These two young men were then about 17 years of age. Boquist's sister, 72 years old, lives in Orebro and attended our meetings. Afterwards she told us about the 1844 movement, and sang for us the hymns her brother sang when he and Walbom were liberated from prison. She had witnessed their whippings with birch rods upon their bare backs. When their wounds were healed, they took them from prison and again demanded, "Will you cease preaching this doctrine?" When they replied, "We will preach the preaching the Lord bids us." they were whipped a second time. Through the intercession of a prominent Orebro lady, hey were liberated by King Oscar I.[2]

The Advent message has advanced with accelerated force and power from year to year, until it has missions encircling the earth. It surely is not because the message is one that is pleasing to carnal hearts that it has prospered; for it carries in its fore-front the Sabbath of the Lord, whose observance requires a separation from business with the world on the busiest day of the week. Neither has it advanced because of no opposition, for this has been encountered from the first, and that of the fiercest kind from without as well as perplexities from within. We may well say with the psalmist, "If it had not been the Lord was on our side, when men rose up against us, then they had swallowed us up quick, when their wrath was kindled against us…. Our help is in the name of the Lord who made heaven and earth." Psalm 124:2, 3, 8.

Not only have we seen the Lord's providence in the rise and progress of the third angel's message, but He has communicated with His people through the gift of prophecy. This has not been in the form of a new revelation to take the place of the Bible, but to show there is danger in departing from the simplicity of the gospel of Christ, becoming satisfied with a form of godliness without the power.

Testing the gift as manifested through Mrs. E. G. White by the Bible rules, we have seen that it stands the test in every particular. In all her writings there has not been found a single line that gives the slightest license to sin, or that tolerates in the least degree any departure from God's Word. These writings have never placed themselves above the Bible, but they constantly exhort to the most careful study of the word of God, pointing to it as the great standard by which our cases will be examined in the final judgment. In the writings, Christ is exalted before us as the only pattern to follow. He is declared to be our only hope of victory here, our only refuge from the wrath to come, and the only name and means through whom we may be saved.

---

2   Loughborough's presentations in Scandinavia were largely devoted to God's guidance in the Advent movement. After his return to America, although he no longer assumed administrative positions, he continued to speak at camp meetings and General Conference sessions. In 1900, he made a tour of Europe, and in 1901, a world tour of Adventist missions, including Europe, Afric, Australia, and New Zealand.

After having watched the matter since 1852, I have found that for the most part the opposition to the gift of prophecy has arisen from those who have been reproved for defects of character, for wrong habits, or for some wrong course in their manner of life. Many of the reproved would protest that they were not as bad as the testimony represented them, but time has shown that the great majority of those who renounced their faith, leave the ranks entirely.

On the other hand, by heeding the counsels given through the spirit of prophecy, and moving forward in the Lord's strength, the message is fast making its way to every nation, and kindred, and tongue, and people. Of the progress in the past we can say that God's Word has been verified, "No weapon formed against thee shall prosper." Truly, the hand of God has been manifest in the success attending the rise and progress of this great Advent movement.

Rural Health Retreat on Howell Mountain near St. Helena, California. In this area Elder Loughborough spent his retirement years, and died in 1924, at the age of 92. On this site now stands the St. Helena Hospital and Health Center.

Sources

Chapter 1

1. *The Advent Review and Sabbath Herald,* January 27, 1891
2. *Pacific Union Recorder*, October 31, 1907.
3. *Pacific Union Recorder*, November 5, 190.7
4. *The Youth's Instructor*, November 1863.
5. *The Advent Review and Sabbath Herald,* January 13, 1891
6. *Pacific Union Recorder,* December 19, 1907.
7. *Pacific Union Recorder,* December 3, 1908.
8. *Pacific Union Recorder,* May 7, 1908.

Chapter 2

1. *The Advent Review and Sabbath Herald,* March 10, 1891; July 30, 1914.
2. *The Youth's Instructor*, January 1864
3. *Pacific Union Recorder,* June 11 and 18, 1908.
4. *The Youth's Instructor*, February 1864.
5. *The Youth's Instructor*, July and August 1864
6. *Pacific Union Recorder,* December 10, 1908.
7. *The Advent Review and Sabbath Herald,* January 29, 1864
8. *Pacific Union Recorder,* December 24, 1908.

Chapter 3

1. *The Youth's Instructor*, January 1865
2. *Pacific Union Recorder,* December 31, 190.8
3. *Pacific Union Recorder,* January 7, 1909.

4. *Pacific Union Recorder,* January 28, 1909.
5. *The Youth's Instructor*, May 1865
6. *Pacific Union Recorder,* February 11, 1909.
7. *The Youth's Instructor*, July 1865.
8. *Good Health*, February 1900.
9. *Pacific Union Recorder,* March 18, 1909; April 8, 1909.
10. *The Advent Review and Sabbath Herald,* February 12, 1884
11. *Pacific Union Recorder,* March 2 and May 1909.

Chapter 4

1. *The Advent Review and Sabbath Herald,* February 12, 1884
2. *Pacific Union Recorder,* April 8, 1909.
3. *Pacific Union Recorder,* May 13, 1909.
4. *Pacific Union Recorder,* July 8 and 15, 1909.
5. *Pacific Union Recorder,* July 29, 1909.
6. *Pacific Union Recorder,* August 12, 1909.

Chapter 5

1. *Pacific Union Recorder,* August 19, 1909.
2. *Pacific Union Recorder,* September 30, 1909.
3. *The Advent Review and Sabbath Herald,* July 31, 1919.
4. *The Advent Review and Sabbath Herald,* June 11, 1901
5. J. N. Loughborough, *The Church, Its Organization, Order and Design* (Review and Herald Publishing Association, 1907), 101.
6. J. N. Loughborough, *Rise and Progress of the Seventh-day Adventists* (General Conference Association of Seventh-day Adventists, 1892), 184–187
7. *Pacific Union Recorder,* November 25, 1909
8. *The Advent Review and Sabbath Herald,* January 15, 1867; June 10, 1884; September 26, 1899.

Chapter 6

1. *Pacific Union Recorder,* January 6, 1910.
2. *Pacific Union Recorder,* January 13, 1910.
3. *Pacific Union Recorder,* February 17, 1910.

4. *Pacific Union Recorder,* March 3, 1910.

5. J. N. Loughborough, *Rise and Progress of the Seventh-day Adventists* (General Conference Association of Seventh-day Adventists, 1892), 199, 200

6. *Pacific Union Recorder,* March 10, 1910.

7. J. N. Loughborough, *Rise and Progress of the Seventh-day Adventists* (General Conference Association of Seventh-day Adventists, 1892), 201

8. J. N. Loughborough, *Great Second Advent Movement* (Nashville: Southern Publishing Association, 1905), 331

9. *Pacific Union Recorder,* April 7, 1910.

Chapter 7

1. *Pacific Union Recorder,* April 14, 1910.

2. *The Advent Review and Sabbath Herald,* August 15, 1854

3. *Pacific Union Recorder,* April 21, 1910.

4. *The Advent Review and Sabbath Herald,* May 24, 1885.

5. *Pacific Union Recorder,* June 30, 1910.

6. *Pacific Union Recorder,* September 16, 1909.

7. Ellen G. White, *Testimonies for the Church*, vol. 1 (Mountain View, CA: Pacific Press Publishing Association, 1868), 143.

8. J. N. Loughborough, *Rise and Progress of the Seventh-day Adventists* (General Conference Association of Seventh-day Adventists, 1892), 203.

9. *The Advent Review and Sabbath Herald,* February 26, 1857

10. *The Advent Review and Sabbath Herald,* March 16, 1886

11. *Pacific Union Recorder,* August 4, 1910.

Chapter 8

1. *The Advent Review and Sabbath Herald,* March 16, 1886

2. *Pacific Union Recorder,* July 7, 1910.

3. *Pacific Union Recorder,* September 1, 1910

4. J. N. Loughborough, *Rise and Progress of the Seventh-day Adventists* (General Conference Association of Seventh-day Adventists, 1892), 212.

5. *Pacific Union Recorder,* September 1, 1910
6. *The Advent Review and Sabbath Herald,* July 16, 1857.
7. *The Advent Review and Sabbath Herald,* October 15, 1857.
8. *Pacific Union Recorder,* September 8, 1910.
9. *Pacific Union Recorder,* February 16, 1911.
10. *Pacific Union Recorder,* September 28, 1911.

Chapter 9

1. *Pacific Union Recorder,* December 14, 1910.
2. J. N. Loughborough, *Rise and Progress of the Seventh-day Adventists* (General Conference Association of Seventh-day Adventists, 1892), 226.
3. J. N. Loughborough, *Rise and Progress of the Seventh-day Adventists* (General Conference Association of Seventh-day Adventists, 1892), 227
4. *Pacific Union Recorder,* December 14, 1910.
5. Ellen G. White, *Testimonies for the Church*, vol. 1 (Mountain View, CA: Pacific Press Publishing Association, 1868), 312.
6. *Pacific Union Recorder,* February 8, 1911, J. N. Loughborough, *Rise and Progress of the Seventh-day Adventists* (General Conference Association of Seventh-day Adventists, 1892), 231–233.
7. *The Advent Review and Sabbath Herald,* September 29, 1899.
8. J. N. Loughborough, *Rise and Progress of the Seventh-day Adventists* (General Conference Association of Seventh-day Adventists, 1892), 238
9. *Pacific Union Recorder,* March 14, 1912.
10. *Pacific Union Recorder* May 23, 1912.
11. J. N. Loughborough, *Rise and Progress of the Seventh-day Adventists* (General Conference Association of Seventh-day Adventists, 1892), 248, 249.
12. Ellen G. White, *Testimonies for the Church*, vol. 1 (Mountain View, CA: Pacific Press Publishing Association, 1868), 427.
13. J. N. Loughborough, *Rise and Progress of the Seventh-day Adventists* (General Conference Association of Seventh-day

Adventists, 1892), 251.

Chapter 10

1. *Pacific Union Recorder,* October 10, 1912.
2. *The Advent Review and Sabbath Herald,* August 5, 1865.
3. *The Advent Review and Sabbath Herald,* September 14, 1865.
4. *The Advent Review and Sabbath Herald,* October 10, 1865.
5. *Pacific Union Recorder,* November 21, 1912.
6. *Pacific Union Recorder,* January 4, 1913.
7. *Pacific Union Recorder,* January 23, 1913.
8. Ellen G. White, *Testimonies for the Church*, vol. 1 (Mountain View, CA: Pacific Press Publishing Association, 1868), 492.
9. *Pacific Union Recorder,* February 20, 1913
10. J. N. Loughborough, *Rise and Progress of the Seventh-day Adventists* (General Conference Association of Seventh-day Adventists, 1892), 263.
11. *Pacific Union Recorder,* April 17, 1913.

Chapter 11

1. *Pacific Union Recorder,* June 19, 1913; July 3, 1913.
2. *Pacific Union Recorder,* January 4, 1906.
3. *Pacific Union Recorder,* February 12, 1911
4. *General Conference Bulletin*, February 12, 1897.
5. *Pacific Union Recorder,* March 19, 1914.
6. *The Advent Review and Sabbath Herald,* March 30, 1869.
7. *Pacific Union Recorder,* April 5 and 12, 1906.
8. *Pacific Union Recorder,* April 19, 1906.
9. *Pacific Union Recorder,* May 3 and 10, 1906.
10. *Pacific Union Recorder,* May 23, 1906.
11. *Pacific Union Recorder,* June 7, 1906.

Chapter 12

1. *Pacific Union Recorder,* June 28, 1906.
2. *Pacific Union Recorder,* March 9, 1906.
3. *Pacific Union Recorder,* August 30, 1906

4. J. N. Loughborough, *Rise and Progress of the Seventh-day Adventists* (General Conference Association of Seventh-day Adventists, 1892), 282–285.

Chapter 13

1. *Pacific Union Recorder,* September 20, 1906
2. *The Advent Review and Sabbath Herald,* June 18, 1872.
3. *Pacific Union Recorder,* October 11, 1906.
4. *The Advent Review and Sabbath Herald,* July 16, 1901
5. *General Conference Bulletin*, March 3, 1899.
6. *Pacific Union Recorder,* October 18, 1906.
7. *The Advent Review and Sabbath Herald,* October 21, 1873
8. *Pacific Union Recorder,* October 25, 1906.
9. *Pacific Union Recorder,* January 8, 1906.
10. *Pacific Union Recorder,* November 1, 1906.
11. *Pacific Union Recorder,* November 8, 1906.
12. Letter from J. N. Loughborough to Willie C. White, January 13, 1880.
13. *Pacific Union Recorder,* January 22, 1906.
14. *Pacific Union Recorder,* November 22 and 29, 1906
15. *The Advent Review and Sabbath Herald,* July 14, 1896.
16. *Pacific Union Recorder,* December 6, 1906
17. J. N. Loughborough, *Rise and Progress of the Seventh-day Adventists* (General Conference Association of Seventh-day Adventists, 1892), 301.
18. *Pacific Union Recorder,* January 10, 1907.
19. *Pacific Union Recorder,* January 17, 1907.
20. *Pacific Union Recorder,* January 24, 1907.

Chapter 14

1. *Pacific Union Recorder,* January 31, 1907.
2. *The Advent Review and Sabbath Herald,* August 22, 1878.
3. *Pacific Union Recorder,* March 21, 1907.
4. J. N. Loughborough, *Rise and Progress of the Seventh-day Adventists* (General Conference Association of Seventh-day

Adventists, 1892), 316

5. *The Advent Review and Sabbath Herald,* January 23, 1879.
6. *The Advent Review and Sabbath Herald,* February 2, 1879, October 24, 1899
7. J. N. Loughborough, *Rise and Progress of the Seventh-day Adventists* (General Conference Association of Seventh-day Adventists, 1892), 320.
8. *Signs of the Times*, September 15, 1881.
9. J. N. Loughborough, *Rise and Progress of the Seventh-day Adventists* (General Conference Association of Seventh-day Adventists, 1892), 330.
10. *Signs of the Times*, January 12, 1882.
11. *Good Health*, January 1883.
12. *The Advent Review and Sabbath Herald,* January 11, 1906.

Chapter 15

13. *General Conference Bulletin*, February 12, 1897.
14. *The Advent Review and Sabbath Herald,* July 14, 1896; July 10, 1906.
15. J. N. Loughborough, *Rise and Progress of the Seventh-day Adventists* (General Conference Association of Seventh-day Adventists, 1892), 383–392.

We invite you to view the complete
selection of titles we publish at:

www.TEACHServices.com

Scan with your mobile
device to go directly
to our website.

Please write or email us your praises, reactions, or
thoughts about this or any other book we publish at:

TEACH Services, Inc.
P U B L I S H I N G
www.TEACHServices.com ● (800) 367-1844

P.O. Box 954
Ringgold, GA 30736

info@TEACHServices.com

TEACH Services, Inc., titles may be purchased in bulk for
educational, business, fund-raising, or sales promotional use.
For information, please e-mail:

BulkSales@TEACHServices.com

Finally, if you are interested in seeing
your own book in print, please contact us at

publishing@TEACHServices.com

We would be happy to review your manuscript for free.

www.ingramcontent.com/pod-product-compliance
Lightning Source LLC
Chambersburg PA
CBHW031602110426
42742CB00036B/686